NOTES FROM A
Swedish Kitchen

NOTES FROM A
Swedish Kitchen

Margareta Schildt Landgren

photography by Tine Guth Linse

First published in 2011 by New Holland Publishers (UK) Ltd
London • Cape Town • Sydney • Auckland

Garfield House
86–88 Edgware Rd
London W2 2EA
United Kingdom

80 McKenzie Street
Cape Town 8001
South Africa

Unit 1
66 Gibbes Street
Chatswood
NSW 2067
Australia

218 Lake Road
Northcote
Auckland
New Zealand

ISBN   978 184773 777 9

Publisher: Clare Sayer
Commissioning Editor: Emma Pattison
Swedish Project Manager: Petra Ward
Translator: Charlotte Merton
Designer: Geoff Borin
Special Photography: Tine Guth Linse
Production: Laurence Poos

10 9 8 7 6 5 4 3 2 1

Reproduction by Pica Digital PTE Ltd, Singapore
Printed and bound in Singapore by Tien Wah Press (PTE) Ltd

Contents

Introduction

I feel enormously privileged to be able to work with the most enjoyable thing I can imagine – food! My life has taken many different directions as I have developed personally and professionally, but food has always been important to me.

My childhood memories are focussed around food and my family gathering to eat my mother's superb, home-cooked meals. Even if I didn't help that much with the cooking at home, because mother's was best, I am certain that my passion for food was born back then. My mother cooked from the basics, which was quite natural in those days. You adjusted what you ate to fit the seasons: it would have been unthinkable to eat, say, strawberries at any time other than summer. We gathered rosehips, blackberries, and mushrooms in the autumn, and made the most of the bounty Nature had to offer. Swedes down the ages have been experts at preserving food for the long, cold winters and making the most of the summer's harvests. It is interesting to see how the old traditions are returning, and that we no longer think it's the norm to import food from all corners of the Earth when they're out of season in Sweden. The autumn's root vegetables, for example, have undergone something of a renaissance in recent years.

My mother, Lisa, really wanted to train as a domestic science teacher, but since there was no such thing as a student loan back in those days, the 10,000 kronor fees were quite beyond the reach of her parents. Instead she was inspired and taught a great deal by her mother-in-law, my grandmother, Ida. Mother later developed her own recipes, and since she was very thorough she even typed them out properly. When she died a couple of years ago I inherited her original recipe book. The three grandchildren all desperately wanted their own copy –

that alone says a great deal. When I look at my mother's recipes it's like a complete family history opening before me – a window into my childhood. The recipe book says so much about past ingredients, cooking methods, traditions and parties. Mother noted down whose favourite recipe it was, and she rewrote it carefully or updated it when needed.

You might think I trained as a domestic science teacher in order to fulfil my mother's dream. In truth, I didn't have the faintest inclination in that direction when I left school, but ended up doing it anyway once I had begun work as a supply teacher. In due course I did indeed train as a domestic science teacher, and loved passing on my passion for food to my pupils. Then I was offered a job in Sockerbolag's test kitchen, where I learned an enormous amount in my four years there, and after that went on to a freelance life as a food writer, author, and filmmaker.

Every time I find myself about to begin a new job, I ask myself what it is I stand for. 'Simple food, cooked from scratch, with locally sourced ingredients' has become my motto. In this book I want to convey a sense of what that might mean in a Swedish kitchen, and to encourage you the reader to cook my recipes, but in your own way. In my family we often cook together, ever since my daughter was little and was able to sit on the kitchen side – an excellent way to spend time together that I hope I can inspire others to try. I often run into people who are apologetic for having covered their copy of my recipe books with food stains: in fact, for a cook, that's one of the greatest possible compliments.

Winter

VINTER

Winter in Sweden

Since Sweden is such a secular country, you might be surprised at just how important the four Sundays in Advent are here. The countdown to Christmas starts on the first Sunday in Advent with the solemn lighting of the first candle in the Advent candlestick, and for many people, church. It's also traditional to turn out en masse to admire the Christmas displays as in the past this was the day shop windows were dressed. Preparations for Christmas begin in earnest, helped along by Christmas markets, Christmas parties, and mulled wine.

The month of December sees a great deal of cooking and baking. Advent has its own special biscuits and cakes, with pride of place going to ginger biscuits and St Lucia buns. I know that Christmas can be stressful for many people, but sometimes I think it's lucky there is such a thing as Christmas once a year, because it gets us to make the extra effort to meet up with good friends and family – something that otherwise never quite happens. People get together over some mulled wine to bake or make Christmas sweets together. I love giving away homemade sweets as Christmas presents. True, the Christmas buffet takes a fair bit of planning as there are so many dishes to be included, but it's also a part of the excitement in the run-up to the big day. There's so much pleasure to be had from thinking out all your favourite dishes and planning the shopping and the cooking. All the Christmas food is so fragrant, evoking a carefree childhood and happy memories. It's probably freshly baked ginger biscuits that spread the most Christmassy of all Christmas perfumes, but when the scent of the Christmas ham in the oven wafts through the house, that's when you know Christmas has finally arrived.

But winter isn't only about Christmas, of course. It's walks in the snowy woods; it's a whole day tobogganing with cocoa in your flask; and it's dreary, grey days of cutting winds and wet snow, when even the cat won't set foot outside, and when you have to cheer yourself up by getting creative in the kitchen. That for me is the moment to turn to baking, experimenting with different types of bread. Whatever bread I produce, it goes well with the rich, warming soups that are very much part of winter, especially since the season's ingredients are so suited to slow cooking. This is the time of year when I always decide that people don't make nearly enough soups – time to give the stockpot a new lease of life!

Köttbullar

MEATBALLS

4 tbsp breadcrumbs
200 g (7 oz) pork mince
200 g (7 oz) beef mince
2 tbsp grated onion
salt and freshly ground
black pepper
butter, for frying

SERVES 4

My mother used to buy a half or whole slaughtered pig that she would use to make brawn, sausages and meatballs. To make meatballs she minced fresh ham and cold boiled potatoes together and froze the mixture in flat patties large enough to make meatballs for the whole family. All she then had to do was take one of the patties out of the freezer, leave it to thaw, roll the mixture into meatballs and fry – easy! So if you have leftover boiled potatoes that need using up, as my mother so often did, substitute them for the breadcrumbs in this recipe.

1 Put the breadcrumbs in a mixing bowl and add 4 tablespoons of cold water. Leave the breadcrumbs to absorb the water for about 5 minutes.

2 Add both minced meats along with the onion and season. Mix until smooth using your hands or a wooden spoon.

3 Roll into meatballs using about 1 tbsp of the mixture at a time. (If you rinse your hands in cold water as you go it's less likely to stick.)

4 Heat the butter in a frying pan and fry the meatballs until golden. Lower the temperature and leave to finish cooking over a low heat for approximately 10 minutes.

5 Serve with lingonberries, boiled or mashed potatoes and Brown Sauce (see page 18).

Steksås

BROWN SAUCE

300 ml (½ pint) boiling water

1 tbsp beef, chicken or
game stock powder (optional)

3 tbsp plain flour

200 ml (⅓ pint) single cream

½ tsp soy sauce

salt and freshly ground
black pepper

SERVES 4

To appreciate the flavour of the meat fully, I think you need to
serve a beef gravy with beef, game gravy with game, chicken gravy
with chicken and so on. However, your sauce or gravy will only
truly complement the dish if you use the cooking juices from the
meat as the basis for your recipe. Ready-made, shop-bought
sauces are just no competition for the real thing. This sauce is the
classic accompaniment to meatballs and if you hear Swedes
ordering brown sauce, this is it.

1 Pour the boiling water into the pan you have been using to cook
your meat and lo and behold, you have delicioius cooking juices to
work with. Add stock powder, if liked, and heat to a simmer.

2 Mix the flour with a little cold water and pour into the
simmering cooking juices in a thin stream, whisking continuously.

3 Pour in the cream and simmer for 5 minutes to allow the flour
to cook. Add the soy sauce and season to taste. Serve with
Meatballs (see page 17) or other meat dishes.

Hasselbackspotatis

HASSELBACK POTATOES

12–15 large potatoes
of a similar size

1 tsp salt

50 g (2 oz) butter

100 g (4 oz) breadcrumbs

SERVES 4

Sometimes it feels as if Hasselback potatoes have been rather forgotten, but every time I produce them to go with roast meat or poultry they receive a warm ovation. This is so satisfying, and it really is the simplest way imaginable to turn a humble potato into a luxurious dish.

1 Preheat the oven to 225°C/425°F/gas 7. Grease a baking sheet or ovenproof dish. Peel the potatoes and cut a thin slice off the bottom of each so they will stand upright. Slice each potato into thin slices taking the knife about ¾ of the way through so that the slices stay together.

2 Put the potatoes on the baking sheet and sprinkle with the salt. Melt the butter and brush it carefully all over the potatoes, retaining a little for use later. Sprinkle with the breadcrumbs and roast for 30–40 minutes, depending on the size of the potatoes, brushing occasionally with the reserved butter.

3 Check the potatoes are cooked through using the point of a knife or a skewer. Serve with roast meat or poultry.

Ärtsoppa

PEA SOUP

1 tbsp salt

500 g (1¼ lb) dried yellow peas

2 litre (3½ pint) vegetable stock

2 onions, chopped

1 tsp fresh thyme

salt and freshly
ground black pepper

200 g (7 oz) smoked pork loin,
finely shredded

SERVES 6

On a cold winter's day a hearty pea soup is the perfect dish. In my family we often have 'pea soup parties' which are traditionally held on Thursdays, and we serve small cups of warm arrack punch (see page 21) to accompany the soup .

1 Dissolve the salt in 2 litres (3½ pints) of cold water. Add the peas and soak for at least 12 hours.

2 Discard the water. Pour the vegetable stock into a saucepan, add the onions and peas and bring to the boil. Cover and simmer over a low heat for 1–1½ hours, or until the peas are soft. Skim occasionally to remove the pea skins.

3 Add the thyme and season to taste. Add the strips of smoked pork loin just before serving. Serve with Arrack Punch (see opposite).

Punsch

ARRACK PUNCH

750 ml (1¼ pints) pure schnapps
or vodka

½ tsp arrack essence

50 ml (2 fl oz) dark rum

330 g (11½ oz) caster sugar or
white baking syrup

MAKES 1 LITRE (1¾ PINTS)

When I was little my father's hunting parties would drink warm arrack punch with their pea soup after a long, chilly day in the field. These days I like to serve it in eggshells with my Egg Flip Parfait (see page 70).

1 Pour all of the liquid ingredients into a large bowl. Add the sugar and mix until dissolved. Pour into sterilized bottles and seal.

2 Leave to mature for 4 weeks before drinking. The punch can be stored for several months.

3 Serve with Pea Soup (see opposite).

Swedish Christmas

I enjoy making my family's absolute favourites to go on our Christmas buffet table, which we set out in all its glory on Christmas Eve. I think it's fun to 'bring in the Yule' with food as well as decorations, and I like to set aside several days for preparing the food, making sweets to give as gifts and baking delicious treats. This way I find the whole run-up to Christmas really enjoyable and not at all onerous. The dishes that are always on our table include Herring in Mustard Sauce (see page 40), Glazier's Herring (see page 38), Christmas Ham (see page 43), Creamed Kale (see page 45), Meatballs (see page 17), homemade Rye Bread (see page 60) and Wholemeal Bread (see pages 63), Gravlax with Gravlax Sauce (see page 77), Mulled Wine (see page 26), My Mother's Ginger Biscuits (see page 30), St Lucia Buns (see page 34), homemade Toffee (see page 37) and Orange Truffles (see page 37). Our table then varies from year to year in the way of sausages, cheeses and other good things to eat.

Glögg
MULLED WINE

150 ml (¼ pint) vodka

6 cinnamon sticks

30 cloves

2 large pieces of dried ginger

a handfull of dried bitter (Seville) orange peel

2 tsp cardamom pods

440 g (15½ oz) granulated sugar

1.5 litres (2½ pints) red wine

MAKES 2 LITRES (3½ PINTS)

Inga-Lill is the mother of my oldest friend. She always made this mulled wine a week before the First of Advent, and we were allowed to taste it when it was ready. Every year I look forward to reliving the taste of my youth! This mulled wine isn't particularly sweet, so add more sugar if you have a sweet tooth.

1 Pour the vodka into a small glass jar. Add the cinnamon, cloves, ginger, orange peel and cardamom. Cover and leave to stand at room temperature for 1 week.

2 Dissolve the sugar in a small amount of the red wine in a saucepan over a low heat. Sieve the vodka to remove the spices. Mix the vodka and sugared wine with the remainder of the red wine.

3 Pour into clean, sterilized bottles – it will keep for several weeks. Heat gently before serving, but don't let it boil.

Christmas biscuits

Every year, at the very beginning of December, my mother would round up me and my brother to help her bake the first batch of Christmas ginger biscuits. This tradition is still very common in many Swedish families and it's certainly something my daughter has grown up with. The biscuits are super thin and crispy and you can easily make 200 in a batch, although I sometimes need to make double to last us until Christmas Eve! It's a bit of a mystery, but as the dough is left to rest in the fridge overnight it tends to shrink, and has lots of little finger marks all over it the following morning. I wonder why... In my family we also make a gingerbread house for Christmas and decorate it with sweets, and every year we seem to acquire a new set of elaborate cookie cutters we have to try out. For kids, decorating with icing is part of the fun but I like ginger biscuits just as they are or with some blue cheese on top, accompanied with a glass of warm Mulled Wine (see page 26).

Lisas pepparkakor

MY MOTHER'S GINGER BISCUITS

150 g (5 oz) butter

150 g (5 oz) caster sugar

150 g (5 oz) golden syrup

1½ tsp ground cloves

1½ tsp ground ginger

1 tsp cinnamon

1 tsp bicarbonate of soda

1 egg

500 g (1¼ lb) plain flour

MAKES ABOUT 200

When I was little my mother mistakenly broke an egg into the ginger biscuit mix. The result was crisp, amazingly good biscuits that we have baked ever since. While they are incredibly easy to make. they can be a bit tricky to roll out, but they are well worth the trouble.

1 Melt the butter, sugar and syrup together in a large saucepan. Mix in the spices and the bicarbonate of soda. Break in the egg, add the flour and mix well. Leave the dough to rest in the fridge overnight.

2 Preheat the oven to 200°C/400°F/gas 6. Roll out the dough very thinly and cut out shapes using biscuit cutters. Bake on a baking sheet in the middle of the oven for 5–7 minutes. Keep an eye on them as they burn very easily.

3 Leave the biscuits to cool on cooling trays. They will keep for up to 4 weeks in an airtight container.

St Lucia

The Lucia celebrations, on the 13th of December, are one of the few Swedish holidays that honour a saint. St Lucia was a Sicilian woman who died a martyr's death in the fourth century, and was patron saint of Syracuse. Today Lucia is celebrated in homes, schools and workplaces across the country, and this is a very important day in Swedish society. Most of the large towns elect their own Lucia, and Swedish television broadcasts the national celebration live very early in the morning. The elected Lucia, wearing a crown of lit candles, leads a white-robed choir in procession, and during her confirmation period my daughter Sara was the Lucia in our church. Like so many other Swedish traditions, Lucia is a mix of Christian and pagan customs. Until 1753, when the Julian calendar was introduced in Sweden, the winter solstice (the longest night of the year) fell on 13 December. People tried to fend off the darkness and the evil forces that roamed free by keeping a candlelit vigil through the night. Today Lucia, an important milestone in the countdown to Christmas, is mostly associated with special children's songs and the fragrant St Lucia buns.

Lussekatter

ST LUCIA BUNS

50 g (2 oz) fresh baker's yeast

150 g (5 oz) butter

500 ml (18 fl oz) milk

a pinch of saffron

1½ tsp salt

135 g (4¾ oz) caster sugar

2 tsp baking powder

900 g (1¾ lb) plain flour

100 g (4 oz) raisins

1 egg

MAKES 32

St Lucia buns are enjoyed throughout Sweden as part of the celebration of St Lucia on 13 December. The tradition of baking and eating these buns comes from a seventeenth-century German legend, which says that Jesus handed out buns to good children while Lucifer, in the shape of a cat, dealt out blows to the bad.

1 Crumble the yeast into a large mixing bowl. Melt the butter in a saucepan, add the milk and warm to body temperature (but no warmer or it will kill the yeast).

2 Pour the milk mixture over the yeast and stir until the yeast has dissolved. Add the saffron, salt and sugar. Mix the baking powder with the flour. Add the flour to the liquid ingredients a little at a time. Mix until the dough is firm and smooth.

3 Leave the dough to rise in a draught-free place at room temperature for 30 minutes. Knock back the dough and knead for around 10 minutes until it's shiny and smooth.

4 Divide the dough into two pieces and roll out each into a thick rectangle. Divide each rectangle in two, and then each of these pieces into 8. Using your fingers, roll out each piece of dough into a long rope-like shape as thick as your finger, and then roll the ends inwards as in the photograph opposite. Place on a baking sheet and press a raisin into the centre of each of the two coils.

5 Leave to prove at room temperature for 30 minutes. Meanwhile preheat the oven to 225°C/425°F/gas 7.

6 Beat the egg in a small bowl or cup and brush the buns with the egg wash. Bake in the middle of the oven for 7–10 minutes until golden brown – the buns sound hollow when you tap them on the bottom. Leave to cool on cooling racks.

Knäck

TOFFEE

150 ml (¼ pint) whipping or double cream

150 ml (¼ pint) golden syrup

150 g (5 oz) granulated sugar

2 tbsp butter

50 g (2 oz) blanched almonds, chopped

MAKES 50 PIECES

Knäck is a very traditional Swedish Christmas sweet. I would argue that there is something seriously missing if I can't stick my teeth into a wonderfully sweet and chewy piece of knäck at Christmas.

1 Mix all of the ingredients, except the almonds, in a thick-bottomed saucepan and simmer for about 45–60 minutes, stirring occasionally.

2 To check if the toffee is ready, spoon a couple of drops of the hot mixture into a glass of cold water. If the mixture holds together and it's possible to roll it into a ball, the toffee is ready. If not, simmer for a little longer. Remove from the heat and stir in the chopped almonds.

3 Spoon into petit four cases and leave in a cool place to set.

Apelsintryffel

ORANGE TRUFFLES

100 ml (3½ fl oz) whipping or double cream

200 g (7 oz) dark chocolate (minimum 70% cocoa)

zest and 1 tbsp juice of an orange

MAKES ABOUT 30

In my family we love to make our own Christmas sweets. These truffles, with their zesty taste of orange, are exceedingly good and they're incredibly quick to make. We often make several batches in pretty cellophane bags to give as gifts when we're invited to mulled wine parties in December.

1 Bring the cream to the boil in a saucepan. Remove from the heat. Break the chocolate into pieces and leave to melt in the cream.

2 Stir the orange juice and a pinch of the zest into the chocolate mix.

3 Spoon the chocolate into petit four cases. Decorate with the remaining orange zest.

4 Leave to set in the fridge for 2 hours. Store in the fridge for 3–4 days.

Glasmästarsill

GLAZIER'S HERRING

400 g (14 oz) salt herring fillets
(see page 41)

1 carrot, sliced

1 red onion, sliced

10 white peppercorns

5 tbsp 12% vinegar essence

100 g (4 oz) granulated sugar

SERVES 3–4 AS A STARTER

My mother carefully layered herring with sliced vegetables and spices in a square glass jar with a cork lid to make this jewelled masterpiece. The unusual name is due to the clear brine which enables all of the ingredients to be seen through the glass jar.

1 Soak the herring fillets in cold water for 6–8 hours, then taste to check they are not too salty. When ready, slice the fish into neat pieces.

2 Layer the herring, carrot, red onion and peppercorns in a pot or glass jar. Pour 150 ml (¼ pint) water into a saucepan. Add the vinegar essence and sugar and bring to the boil. Pour the hot brine over the herring.

3 Leave to stand in the fridge for at least 3 days before serving. Serve cold with boiled potatoes or as part of a smörgåsbord.

Senapssill

HERRING IN MUSTARD SAUCE

3 tbsp sweetish mustard

3 tbsp caster sugar

1 tsp salt

3 tbsp rapeseed oil

3 tbsp sour cream

handful of dill, finely chopped

400 g (14 oz) salt herring fillets
(see page 41), sliced

SERVES 3–4 AS A STARTER

There are a couple of pickled herring dishes I absolutely must have on my Christmas buffet, and this is one of them. Here is my version of herring in mustard sauce that is much appreciated both by herring fanatics and those who usually opt out. Delicious.

1 Mix the mustard, sugar and salt together in a mixing bowl. Whisk in the oil and then fold in the sour cream.

2 Mix in the dill and the herring and decant into a lidded pot or glass jar. Leave for at least 6 hours in the fridge before serving. The herring will keep for about 1 week in the fridge.

3 Serve cold on brown bread, with boiled potatoes or as part of a smörgåsbord.

Saltad Sill

SALT HERRING

2 kg (4½ lb) whole,
fresh herring with heads
and gills removed

600 g (1½ lb) coarse salt

Salt herring is the basis of most Swedish pickled herring dishes. It is traditional to eat salt herring unadorned – just salted – but the fish are far too salty for most of us these days. The weights given here are for whole herring with heads and gills removed. Once the process is complete, and you've gutted and filleted the fish, you'll need to reweigh the fillets to gauge how much you need for your intended recipe. Salt herring are ideal for recipes such as Glazier's Herring (see page 38) and Herring in Mustard Sauce (see page 40), and you'll find you have a little left over to experiment with your own flavours and dressings.

1 Place the prepared herring and the salt into a jar or pot with a tightly-fitting lid. Seal and leave to stand in a cool place or in the refrigerator for at least a fortnight.

2 Before use soak the salt herring in water – for 2 herring use 3 litres (5¼ pints). Leave in a cool place for at least 24 hours, then drain.

3 Gut and fillet the herring and rinse well in cold water. The salt herring is now ready for use in your chosen recipe.

Christmas ham

Place of honour on a Swedish Christmas buffet is always taken by the Christmas ham – a big, salt-cured ham that has been boiled or baked. Boiling the ham means you can make *dopp i grytan* (sops in broth), a much-loved Christmas dish which involves dunking coarse rye bread or wort-bread in the salty, fatty broth in which the ham was cooked.

The tradition of eating ham at Christmas goes back to pre-Christian times, and can be traced to Nordic mythology. In Valhalla the Aesir, the principal gods, gathered to feast every night on Särimner the boar, who was then brought back to life by collecting together the chewed bones after the meal, ready for the following day. In old peasant communities it was a matter of pride and status to be able to have a large ham at Christmas, and they made sure the pig was well fed. The meat was used in a multitude of dishes that would keep well, such as sausages, meatballs, brawn or salt pork.

Julskinka

CHRISTMAS HAM

5 kg (11 lb) fresh ham
on the bone

DAY 1

6 tbsp table salt

3 tbsp granulated sugar

1 tbsp saltpetre
(potassium nitrate)

DAY 2

6 tbsp granulated sugar

6 tsp saltpetre
(potassium nitrate)

1.5 kg (3 lb) coarse salt

TO FINISH

1 egg

1 tbsp granulated sugar

3 tbsp mild mustard

50 ml (2 fl oz) breadcrumbs

The Christmas ham is the high point of any Christmas spread in Sweden. When I was a child we always ordered a fresh ham from a good pig farmer, and then cured it from scratch. Just remember to start in good time if you want to try the ham before the big day.

DAY 1 Mix the day 1 ingredients together and rub into the ham. Leave to stand in the fridge overnight.

DAY 2 Dissolve the sugar, saltpetre and coarse salt in 6 litres (10½ pints) of water to make a brine. Pour into a saucepan and bring to the boil. Place the ham into a pot or bowl just large enough to hold it and the brine. Pour the hot brine over the ham. Leave the ham to stand in the brine in a cool place for a fortnight.

DAY 16 Discard the brine, place the ham in a saucepan of fresh, cold water to cover, and bring to the boil over a low heat. Simmer until a meat thermometer reads 75°–80°C, which will take 2–3 hours. Leave the ham to cool in the liquid.

TO FINISH Preheat the oven to 200°C/400°F/gas 6. Beat the egg with the sugar and mustard. Brush the egg mix onto the ham and sprinkle over the breadcrumbs. Bake the ham in the oven for about 15 minutes until it is golden in colour. Slice once it has cooled slightly and serve.

Janssons frestelse

JANSSON'S TEMPTATION

200 g (7 oz) Swedish ansjovis

2 onions, finely sliced

1 kg (2 lb) floury potatoes, peeled and cut into fine batons

freshly ground pepper

300 ml (½ pint) double cream

3 tbsp breadcrumbs

2 tbsp butter

TO SERVE

tomatoes and cucumber, sliced

SERVES 4

Jansson's temptation is the most delicious fish dish I can imagine. It doesn't look like much, but once the creamy potatoes have married with the ansjovis, appearances don't really matter any more. It is perfect on a smörgåsbord or Christmas buffet, or as a light supper or simple lunch. Do keep in mind that Swedish ansjovis are not the same as canned sprats or anchovies – they have a certain mix of spices that are important in this dish.

1 Preheat oven to 200°C/400°F/gas 6. Butter a large, shallow ovenproof dish. Layer the fish, onions and potatoes in the dish. Season with pepper and pour over two thirds of the cream. Sprinkle over the breadcrumbs and dot with the butter.

2 Bake in the lower part of the oven for about 45 minutes until the surface is golden and the potato is soft. If the dish appears dry during cooking, add the remaining cream. Serve with sliced tomatoes and cucumber.

Långkål

CREAMED KALE

3 litres (5¼ pints) ham or vegetable stock

800 g (1¾ lb) kale, stripped from its stalks

2 tbsp butter

100 ml (3½ fl oz) double cream

salt and freshly ground black pepper

SERVES 6–8

My family comes from Skåne, the southernmost province of Sweden, where it's traditional to have browned cabbage as part of the Christmas buffet, but we have always had this creamed kale from the neighbouring province of Halland as well. The kale makes a nice contrast to all the salty, fatty Christmas food. I buy the beautiful kale fronds after the first frosts, and then it's time to strip the kale from its stalks, rinse it, boil it and chop it for all I'm worth.

1 Bring the ham or vegetable stock to the boil in a large saucepan. Add the kale, a little at a time as it collapses rapidly, and simmer for 30 minutes.

2 Drain off the stock (you can save it to make kale soup later). Chop the kale. Melt the butter in a large frying pan, tip in the kale, and sizzle.

3 Pour over the cream and simmer until it's reduced to a thick sauce. Season to taste.

4 Serve the creamed kale as part of a Christmas buffet, or eat it with slices of Christmas Ham (see page 43).

Julkorv.

3,0 kg. oxkött,	2,5 kg.	fläskspäck
3,0 " fläskkött,	4,0 "	kokt,kall potatis
4,0 l. kokt kall mjölk,	15 msk.	salt
4 msk. salpeter ,	2 1/2 msk.	vitpeppar
1 1/2 msk. starkpeppar ,	1 1/2 "	ingfära
1,0 " kryddpeppar ,	3 "	socker.

Beredning: Köttmassan arbetas väl ,under tillsats
av kryddorna och mjölken i små mängder.
När smeten verkar pösig och jämn inarbetas

späcket och potatisen under en kortare stund.
Smeten fylles i väl rengjorda fjälster.
Av denna sats blir det 12,0 kg. korv.

Korven ingnides i tre dygn med 2 msk. salt,
1 msk. socker , 1 tsk. salpeter.

Rökas därefter i 2,0 timmar.

Detta är Henrys " Älsklingskorv. "

Christmas sausages

My mother used to buy half a pig, fresh from slaughter, a couple of times a year, and when my daughter Sara was little she sometimes helped granny make *bräckekorv*, or sausages for frying. Sara had no idea what a sausage casing was, but drawing on her nursery school experience of various viscous materials she settled on 'slime'. After we had stuffed our own sausages we used to take them to a smokery where you could pick a type of wood, such as oak or beech, to flavour the meat. For children *prinskorvar*, small smoked sausages quite similar to a Frankfurter in taste, are obligatory on the Swedish Christmas smörgåsbord and you would have groans of disappointment if they were left out.

Making your own sausages might seem messy but it's great fun. If you've got a Kitchen Aid at home, check if it has a sausage attachment. I've noticed a new trend when it comes to traditional bangers – more and more people want to try out their own versions with more adventurous flavours, high meat content and no additives.

Risgrynsgröt och Ris à la Malta

RICE PUDDING AND RICE CREAM PUDDING

150 g (5 oz) pudding rice

1 tsp salt

700 ml (1¼ pint) whole milk

1 cinnamon stick

1½ tbsp caster sugar

RICE CREAM PUDDING

150 ml (¼ pint) whipping cream

1 tbsp caster sugar

2 tsp vanilla sugar

TO SERVE

1 blanched almond (optional)

Blackberry Preserve (see page 202) or fresh berries

SERVES 4

Hot rice pudding is traditionally served at Christmas in Sweden. Rice cream pudding, a cold version, has a creaminess that works perfectly when combined with the sharpness of the berries. Traditionally, a blanched almond is stirred into the finished pudding. Whoever gets the almond in their serving will get married, or at least meet their true love, the following year.

If you cook this dish for Christmas Eve and have a bit left over, you should definitely leave out a bowl of it for Father Christmas. His taste differs from country to country, but in Sweden he likes finding a bowl of rice pudding on the front doorstep.

1 Place the rice and salt in a saucepan. Add 300 ml (½ pint) of water and bring to the boil. Cover and simmer for 10 minutes.

2 Add the milk and cinnamon stick. Mix well. Cover and leave the pudding on a very low heat until the rice has absorbed the milk, which will take about 30 minutes. The pudding will burn very easily, so be careful to have the heat as low as possible.

3 Stir in the sugar and leave the pudding to cool until it is lukewarm (if served warm), or until it is cold (if served as rice cream pudding).

4 For rice cream pudding, whip the cream, mix in the caster sugar and vanilla sugar and mix with the cold rice.

5 Add the blanched almond, if you wish, and serve with a preserve such as the Blackberry Preserve on page 202 or fresh berries.

Saftsås

FRUIT CORDIAL SAUCE

500 ml (18 fl oz) strong diluted
raspberry cordial

1 tbsp potato flour
or cornflour

100 g (4 oz) raspberries

sugar, to taste

SERVES 4

Fruit cordial sauce is the perfect accompaniment for Christmas rice pudding. I don't like to make it too sweet, otherwise it doesn't contrast as well with the pudding. Add more sugar if you prefer.

1 Pour the diluted cordial into a saucepan and whisk in the potato flour or cornflour.

2 Bring to the boil, stirring continuously, until it just begins to bubble (do not overcook as the potato flour will make the sauce gluey).

3 Finally stir in the raspberries and sugar. Serve the sauce lukewarm with Rice Pudding and Rice Cream Pudding (see page 48) or Curd Cake (see page 54).

Nötchokladrutor

CHOCOLATE NUT SQUARES

75 g (3 oz) plain flour

½ tsp baking powder

100 g (4 oz) butter

165 g (5½ oz) caster sugar

1 egg

2 tbsp cocoa powder

1 tsp vanilla sugar

150 g (5 oz) hazelnuts, chopped

MAKES 30

These little cakes are so simple to bake. Of all the sweet things to go with a cup of coffee, these are my favourite. It's something of a Swedish classic, and there's life in the old recipe yet.

1 Preheat the oven to 200°C/400°F/gas 6. Mix the flour and baking powder together in a mixing bowl. In a seperate bowl beat together the butter, sugar and egg until fluffy. Add the cocoa and vanilla sugar to the egg mixture, and then fold in the flour.

2 Line a 25 x 35 cm (10 x 13¾ in) baking tin with baking parchment and grease well. Pour in the mixture.

3 Sprinkle over the hazelnuts. Bake in the middle of the oven for about 10–12 minutes.

4 Remove from the oven and immediately cut into 30 squares. Leave to cool in the tin.

Chokladbollar

CHOCOLATE BALLS

100 g (4 oz) cold butter

85 g (3¼ oz) caster sugar

3 tbsp good cocoa powder

120 g (4½ oz) rolled oats

50 g (2 oz) desiccated coconut

MAKES 30–40

When I was growing up, like many other Swedish children I loved to make chocolate balls. I still think they can be absolutely delicious, but they do have to be homemade. I cannot imagine ever buying chocolate balls. I don't think they taste nearly as good as those you can make at home, and, besides, they're always far too big. I make them teeny tiny!

1 Mix together the butter, sugar, cocoa and rolled oats.

2 Spread the desiccated coconut on a plate. Using your hands, roll the mixture into small chocolate balls and then roll them in the coconut. Leave to set in the fridge.

Ostkaka

CURD CAKE

3 eggs

85 g (3¼ oz) caster sugar

150 ml (¼ pint) double cream

150 ml (¼ pint) milk

500 g (1½ lb) cottage cheese

100 g (4 oz) blanched almonds, chopped

TO SERVE

jam or Fruit Cordial Sauce (see page 49)

SERVES 4

Curd cake is usually eaten as a pudding or a snack. It originates from the southern province of Småland, where it is traditionally made using rennet. However, I want to sing the praises of curd cake made using cottage cheese, and so have used this ingredient instead.

1 Preheat the oven to 175°C/350°F/gas 4. Grease a 20 x 30 cm (8 x 11¾ in) ovenproof dish. Beat the eggs and sugar together until thick and pale. Mix in the cream and milk.

2 Fold in the cottage cheese and chopped almonds. Pour into the ovenproof dish and bake for 50–60 minutes until the curd cake has set slightly.

3 Serve lukewarm with jam or Fruit Cordial Sauce (see page 49).

Nöttoppar

HAZELNUT MACAROONS

250 g (9 oz) hazelnuts
50 g (2 oz) butter
110 g (4¼ oz) caster sugar
½ tsp vanilla sugar
1 egg

MAKES ABOUT 25

Macaroons are among my absolute favourite sweet treats. Even if you've never baked them before, I can pretty much guarantee that they'll be a resounding success.

1 Preheat the oven to 175°C/350°F/gas 4. Line a baking sheet with baking parchment.

2 Reserve 25 hazelnuts as decoration. Chop the remainder finely in a food processor.

3 Mix the butter, sugar, vanilla sugar, egg and chopped hazelnuts together until smooth. Drop spoonfuls of the mixture onto the baking sheet, topping each with a whole hazelnut.

4 Bake in the middle of the oven for about 15 minutes, but keep an eye on them so they don't burn. Leave to cool on a cooling rack.

Semlor

LENT BUNS

50 g (2 oz) fresh baker's yeast

100 g (4 oz) butter

400 ml (14 fl oz) milk

110 g (4¼ oz) caster sugar or white baking syrup

a pinch of salt

1 tsp baking powder

1 kg (2 lb) plain flour

1 egg, beaten

200 g (7 oz) Coarse Almond Paste (see page 58) or marzipan

200 ml (⅓ pint) whipping or double cream

3 tbsp icing sugar

MAKES 24

I'm in two minds about the fact that Lent buns can be bought straight after Christmas these days. Traditionally they should only be eaten on Shrove Tuesday, the Tuesday before the first Sunday in Lent (hence their alternative name, Shrove Tuesday buns) – and that's it! A tip from my time working in Sockerbolaget's (the Swedish sugar company's) test kitchen: try using white baking syrup instead of sugar. And go easy on the flour, as it makes for a fluffier bun.

1 Crumble the yeast into a large mixing bowl. Melt the butter in a saucepan. Add the milk and warm to blood temperature. Pour the milk mixture over the yeast and stir until the yeast has dissolved.

2 Add the sugar and salt. Mix the baking powder with the flour. Add the flour, a little at the time, mixing well after each addition until the dough is firm and smooth. Cover with a clean cloth and leave to rise at room temperature for about 30 minutes.

3 Knock back and knead dough until it is shiny and elastic. Roll out to a thick rope shape and divide into 24 evenly sized pieces. Roll each piece in turn on a work surface using your cupped hand until it forms a smooth bun, then place on a baking sheet lined with baking parchment. Leave to prove for a further 30 minutes covered with a clean cloth. Meanwhile preheat the oven to 225°C/425°F/gas 7.

4 Brush the buns with beaten egg, and then bake in the middle of the oven for 6–8 minutes until golden brown.

5 Leave to cool wrapped in a clean tea towel on cooling rack. Slice the almond paste and whip the cream.

6 Once the buns have cooled, slice off a lid from each. Place a slice of almond paste on the bottom half, top with a dollop of cream and then replace the lid. Dust with icing sugar and serve immediately.

Mandelmassa

COARSE ALMOND PASTE

200 g (7 oz) blanched
almonds

60 g (2¼ oz) icing sugar

110 g (4¼ oz) caster sugar

MAKES 370 G (13 OZ)

This almond paste is a wonderful ingredient used in many Swedish pastries. It's very close to marzipan in taste, but has a coarser texture and contains more almonds than sugar. It is possible to buy ready-made *mandelmassa*, but it is extra nice if you can make your own. Try grating it over a fruit tart or using it as a filling in Lent Buns (see page 56).

1 Whiz the almonds in a food processor until they are finely ground but not oily. Add both sugars and mix to a firm consistency. A few drops of cold water may be needed to bring it together.

2 Roll into a large sausage shape and wrap in cling film. Store in the refrigerator until ready to use.

Surdegskultur

SOUR DOUGH STARTER

DAY 1, EVENING

150 ml (¼ pint) lukewarm water

1 tsp honey

135 g (4¾ oz) rye flour

DAY 2, MORNING

100 ml (3½ fl oz) lukewarm water

70 g (2¾ oz) rye flour

DAY 2, EVENING

100 ml (3½ fl oz) lukewarm water

70 g (2¾ oz) rye flour

DAY 3, MORNING

100 ml (3½ fl oz) lukewarm water

70 g (2¾ oz) rye flour

MAKES ENOUGH FOR 1 LARGE OR 2 SMALL LOAVES

Sour dough bread has had something of a renaissance in recent years. The method is perfectly suited to the coarser loaves that are so popular in Scandinavia. I've heard of sour dough recipes that have been passed down through several generations of the same family. If you make a sour dough starter, after three days you'll have a 'ferment' to bake superb bread with.

1 On the evening of day 1, rinse out a mixing bowl with boiling water to speed up the fermentation process. Mix the lukewarm water, honey and rye flour together in the bowl and cover with cling film. Place the bowl in a warm, draught-free place and leave to stand.

2 The following morning, rinse out a larger mixing bowl with boiling water. Place the starter into the clean bowl and 'feed' it with the lukewarm water and rye four. Mix well. Repeat this process in the evening and the following morning. The culture is ready when it has a faint sour scent and bubbles slightly.

3 To keep the culture alive, store it in a cool place and add 35 g (1¼ oz) rye flour and 100 ml (3½ fl oz) lukewarm water once a week, and 1 tsp honey once a month.

Rågbröd

RYE BREAD

DAY 1

100 ml (3½ fl oz) sour dough starter (see page 59)

140 g (4¾ oz) rye flour

200 ml (⅓ pint) lukewarm water

DAY 2

500 ml (18 fl oz) lukewarm water

1 tsp salt

500 g (1¼ lb) rye flour

425 g (15 oz) plain flour

MAKES 1 LARGE OR 2 SMALL LOAVES

Baking bread is so rewarding. There are endless numbers of recipes to try out and every country in the world has its specialities. For a little inspiration I often visit David Fernandes (pictured opposite) at Pâtisserie David in my home town of Malmö. He makes the most wonderful bread imaginable which I buy when I don't have time to bake bread myself.

I am a bit of a periodical baker when it comes to baking sour dough bread. Sometimes I have a sour dough starter ready and waiting to be used, but if I take a break and go over to baking wholemeal bread, when I get round to baking sour dough again I just have to start over, and plan three days in advance...

DAY 1 Put the sour dough starter in a mixing bowl and add half of the rye flour and half of the water. Mix well, cover with cling film and leave at room temperature for 5 hours. Add the remaining rye flour and water. Mix well, cover with cling film and leave to stand overnight.

DAY 2 The following morning add the lukewarm water, salt and rye flour. Finally add the plain flour and knead until the dough is firm and smooth. Cover and leave to rise at room temperature for 1 hour. Knock the dough back and knead until it is smooth and shiny. Shape into one large or two small loaves and leave to prove on a baking sheet for 30 minutes.

Meanwhile preheat the oven to 250°C/475°F/gas 9. Bake for 10 minutes then lower the oven temperature to 225°C/450°F/gas 8 and bake for a further 30 minutes, or until the crust is golden and the loaves sound hollow when the bottom is tapped. Cover with a clean cloth and leave to cool on a cooling rack.

Fullkornsbröd

WHOLEMEAL BREAD

50 g (2 oz) fresh baker's yeast

1 litre (1¾ pints) milk

100 ml (3½ fl oz) cold water

1 tsp salt

75 g (3 oz) linseed, sunflower seeds or chopped walnuts (optional)

500 g (1¼ lb) rye, chopped

300 g (11 oz) wholemeal flour

600 g (1 lb 5 oz) plain flour

MAKES 3 LOAVES

In my late teens I used to spend the summer holidays with my best friend and her family at the summer house in Ala on the Baltic island of Gotland. Her mother always baked this wholemeal bread. It doesn't have to be kneaded, you just splot the porridgey dough straight into the loaf tins. In my family we bake it for breakfast. I like to vary the flavourings as the fancy takes me – linseed, sunflower seeds, or walnuts all make for delicious bread.

My wholemeal bread is in the basket in the photograph opposite, and a loaf of my delicious home-baked Rye Bread (see page 60) can be seen on the chopping board.

1 Grease and flour 3 loaf tins. Crumble the yeast into a mixing bowl or kitchen mixer. Warm the milk until it's lukewarm then pour onto the yeast along with the water.

2 Stir in the salt, any seeds or nuts, the chopped rye and wholemeal flour, and finally the plain flour. Scoop the sticky dough into the prepared tins.

3 Leave to prove for 1 hour at room temperature. Meanwhile preheat the oven to 225°C/450°F/gas 8.

4 Bake the bread in the lower part of the oven for 30 minutes, then cover with aluminium foil and bake for a further 30 minutes.

5 Turn out the bread immediately and leave to cool under a clean tea towel.

Spring
VÅR

Spring in Sweden

Finally the evenings are lighter and the days start to get longer. The first flowers struggle up through the last of the grubby, icy snow. Not long after the crocuses appear, tempting you think that spring must be just around the corner. And then there's another fall of snow, and it seems as if the slush will never end. We Swedes follow the battle between the grip of winter and the arrival of spring with eager expectation. Local newspapers report on the first signs of spring and give the times for sunrise and sunset. Soon enough the blackbirds are singing in the spring twilight, and the forest slopes are covered with bright wood anemones. I always like to gather some of these delicate harbingers of spring as a way of marking the passing of the seasons.

In springtime it's thrilling to go to market again. By Easter it's usually in full swing, and it's such a joy to see the small stalls selling wonderful fresh eggs straight from the farm, perhaps alongside small, carefully tied bunches of spring flowers. Easter brings the first family traditions of the year, and on Good Friday we decorate eggs and set out an Easter buffet. After the long winter we are longing for light, clean-tasting dishes with lots of beautiful spring vegetables. If I had to choose my absolute favourites, they would have to be nettles, asparagus and rhubarb. Nettles come first, and it's exhilarating to set off outdoors to pick them, while their exquisite flavour sings out in so many dishes. When I see the first bundles of freshly cut asparagus at the greengrocers I'm overjoyed! Few things can match the perfection of that first bite into a tender asparagus tip. And then there's the rhubarb – suddenly it's there, presiding in glorious state over the kitchen garden. After months of stodgy puddings, rhubarb's acidity is more than welcome. I like to pick one of the flowering stalks to have in a tall vase in the house – a very elegant tribute to spring.

Swedish Easter

Easter is a pretty big event in Sweden, and the celebrations have both Christian and pagan origins. Branches of birch are put in a vase and decorated with hanging ornaments in Easter-like colours and shapes, and old fairytales tell stories of how witches would fly on their broomsticks to meet the devil for a night of dancing on the Thursday before Easter. On this day you will see lots of children dressed up as (rather sweet and harmless) witches to deliver Easter greeting cards to neighbours in return for sweets. In my house we have almost as many Easter decorations as we have for Christmas. In addition to all the craft projects brought home from school, I have over the years accumulated an interesting collection of egg cups that will have their yearly outing at Easter.

In Sweden it is always the evening before the actual holiday that sees the start of the celebrations. These 'eves' aren't actually holidays as such, but they still count as important days in the calendar. So don't be surprised if you are confronted by Easter eggs on Easter Saturday rather than Easter Sunday, and Christmas presents on Christmas Eve instead of Christmas Day.

Äggtoddyparfait

EGG FLIP PARFAIT

4 egg yolks
(reserve the egg shells)

4 tbsp caster sugar

½ tsp vanilla sugar

200 ml (⅓ pint) whipping or
double cream

TO SERVE

fruit juice, Arrack Punch (see
page 21) or brandy

SERVES 4

I grew up with the idea that everyone should whisk up their own egg flip in a glass just before Easter dinner. As children we flavoured ours with orange juice, and the adults used Arrack Punch (see page 21) or brandy. These days I make egg flip parfait for Easter dinner dessert, and it is always a great success.

1 Wash the reserved egg shells and remove any membrane from the insides.

2 Beat the egg yolks, sugar and vanilla sugar together until thick and pale. Whip the cream separately and then fold the cream carefully into the egg mix.

3 Pour into 4 ramekins and freeze for at least 3 hours.

4 Remove from the freezer 10–15 minutes before serving. Place an egg shell in each portion and pour the fruit juice, arrack punch or brandy into the shell. Serve immediately.

Herring

Herring is probably the world's most common fish. Historically, the supply of herring has been extremely important to Sweden. Along the west coast there are legends of herring shoals so large that the fishermen could wade in the shallows with fish up to their knees, while at other times the herring seemed to have vanished completely. Herring still plays a central role in Swedish festive food. It is pickled with various combinations of spices, herbs and accompaniments and there is some kind of herring on the table at nearly every holiday. Amongst the most popular is mattie herring (see Mattie Herring Tart on page 74), which has a spice mix that includes allspice berries, cloves, sugar and cinnamon. Mattie herring originally comes from the Netherlands, the Swedish name originating from the Dutch *maatjesharing*, or 'virgin herring'.

Matjessilltårta

MATTIE HERRING TART

300 g (11 oz) Swedish *kavring*
or other dark rye bread

50 g (2 oz) butter

3 leaves of gelatine

250 g (9 oz) mattie herring fillets

1 bunch chives

300 ml (½ pint) crème fraîche

200 ml (⅓ pint) quark

50 g (2 oz) lumpfish roe

SERVES 8

This tart is a good dish for an Easter buffet, but is also great as a midsummer dish or as a starter at any time of year. A *smörgåstårta*, a massive savoury 'sandwich-cake', is a uniquely Swedish way to feed a crowd, but I prefer serving a large mattie herring tart at a party as the salty, spicy herring balances beautifully with the dark, slightly sweet flavours of the bread. Mattie herring can be bought from specialist Swedish food stores.

1 Whizz the bread to fine crumbs in a food processor. Melt the butter and mix well into the breadcrumbs.

2 Press the crumb mix into a 24 cm (9½ in) loose-bottomed cake tin. Soak the gelatine in a little cold water for 5 minutes. Chop the mattie herring.

3 Reserve a few chive stalks for decoration and chop the remainder finely. Mix together the crème fraîche, quark, herring and chopped chives.

4 Squeeze the gelatine to remove the excess water and melt in a small saucepan over a low heat. Fold it into the herring mixture, working carefully to avoid lumps forming.

5 Pour the filling mixture over the bread base and refrigerate for at least four hours, preferably overnight.

6 Decorate with the lumpfish roe and the reserved chives.

Dillstuvad potatis

POTATOES IN DILL CREAM SAUCE

10 medium waxy potatoes,
peeled

2 tbsp butter

3 tbsp plain flour

200 ml (⅓ pint) whipping cream

200 ml (⅓ pint) milk

salt and freshly ground
black pepper

1 bunch fresh dill,
finely chopped

SERVES 4

Potatoes in dill cream sauce served with gravlax (see the photograph on page 76) have become a real classic for a good reason. Choose waxy potatoes rather than floury ones or they will disintegrate into mash, and be generous with the richly flavoured dill.

1 Boil the potatoes in lightly salted water until just cooked. Drain and leave to steam dry, and then leave them to go cold. If you can, cook the potatoes the day before and leave in the fridge overnight.

2 Melt the butter in a saucepan. Whisk in the flour over the heat until there are no lumps. Pour in the cream and whisk well. Add the milk, a little at a time, and then simmer for 5 minutes, stirring continuously. Make sure you stir right into the corners of the pan as the mixture will burn easily. Season with salt and pepper.

3 Slice the potatoes and mix with the cream sauce. Just before serving fold in the dill.

Örtgravad lax

GRAVLAX WITH HERBS

1 kg (2 lb) frozen side of fresh
salmon with skin

2 tbsp chopped dill

2 tbsp chopped parsley

1 tbsp chopped tarragon

1 tbsp chopped basil

100 g (4 oz) granulated sugar

75 g (3 oz) salt

freshly ground black pepper

SERVES 4–6

When you get the opportunity, buy half a side of fresh salmon and freeze it ready to make your own gravlax. It is so much tastier and cheaper than buying it ready-made, and simple to make too. Here the salmon is flavoured with herbs, but do try using other flavours such as fennel seeds or crushed juniper berries. Serve the gravlax with Potatoes in Dill Cream Sauce (see page 75) and Gravlax Sauce (below).

1 The salmon must be frozen for at least 24 hours before you begin. Remove from the freezer and leave to thaw in the fridge.

2 Remove all bones, including all the pin bones. Mix the remaining ingredients in a bowl and spread over the salmon. Cover with cling film and refrigerate for 24 hours. Turn the salmon and refrigerate a further 24 hours.

3 Scrape off most of the herbs, slice thinly and serve.

Gravlaxsås

GRAVLAX SAUCE

6 tbsp sweetish mustard

2 tbsp white wine vinegar

3 tbsp golden caster sugar

salt and freshly ground
black pepper

200 ml (⅓ pint) good olive oil

1 bunch fresh dill,
finely chopped

SERVES 6

Gravlax sauce is the ideal accompaniment for gravlax, but it is also good with fresh crab in the autumn.

1 Mix the mustard, vinegar, sugar, salt and pepper together in a bowl. Whisk in the oil in a fine stream so that the sauce thickens. Finally stir in the dill.

2 The sauce is even better if it is left to mature for a day or so in the fridge before serving.

Nässelsoppa

NETTLE SOUP

3 good handfuls of nettle tops

2 tbsp butter

3 tbsp plain flour

1 litre (1¾ pints) vegetable stock

100 ml (3½ fl oz) single cream

100 g (4 oz) smoked salmon, finely sliced

100 ml (3½ fl oz) crème fraîche

SERVES 4

First out into Mother Nature's larder to pick tender young nettle tops. Then home feeling chilly but virtuous to blanch them quickly and cook this scrumptious, vitamin-rich nettle soup.

1 Rinse the nettles and blanch them in 300 ml (½ pint) lightly salted water. Drain, reserving the cooking water, and chop.

2 Melt the butter in a saucepan and stir in the flour, whisking well to remove any lumps. Whisk in the cooking water, vegetable stock and cream. Simmer for 5 minutes then add the nettles.

3 Stir the salmon into the crème fraîche. Serve the soup with a dollop of the salmon mixture in each bowl.

Nässelsufflé

NETTLE SOUFFLÉ

1 tbsp breadcrumbs

50 g (2 oz) butter, plus extra for greasing

5 tbsp plain flour

300 ml (½ pint) milk

6 eggs

2 good handfuls of nettles, blanched and chopped

salt and freshly ground black pepper

a pinch of grated nutmeg

SERVES 4

It's around Easter time that the first nettles start to appear. That's when we dig out our gardening gloves and pick the nettle tops, when the leaves are no bigger than a mouse's ear. It's worth picking masses when you have the chance, blanching them and storing in the freezer for use later. This elegant soufflé is wonderful with smoked salmon or gravlax.

1 Preheat the oven to 175°C/350°F/gas 4. Grease a 1.5 litre (2½ pint) soufflé dish, a tall straight-sided ovenproof dish, or four large ramekins. Coat the inside of the dish or ramekins with the breadcrumbs.

2 Melt the butter in a saucepan. Gradually add the flour and the milk, stirring continuously to make a thick roux. Simmer for 5 minutes, stirring regularly so that it doesn't burn.

3 Remove the saucepan from the heat. Separate the eggs, place the whites in one mixing bowl and the yolks in another.

4 Beat the egg yolks into the roux one by one. Squeeze the nettles as much as possible to remove any excess water and add to the roux, Season and add the nutmeg. Beat the egg whites until stiff and fold into the nettle roux.

5 Pour into the prepared dish or ramekins and bake in the oven for about 30 minutes, or until the soufflé is firm and the top is golden brown. Serve immediately or the soufflé will collapse.

Grillad sparris med nöt- och ostsmak

ASPARAGUS WITH HAZELNUT VINAIGRETTE AND CHEESE CRUMBS

7 tbsp butter

2 tbsp balsamic vinegar

4 tbsp hazelnuts, finely chopped

2 slices of day-old white bread

100 g (4 oz) Västerbotten cheese (a mature Cheddar would also work well)

2 bundles green asparagus (about 30 spears)

salt and freshly ground black pepper

SERVES 4

I like to eat the first tender spears of asparagus raw with a cheese and avocado dip – a lovely nibble with a glass of good wine. The later cuttings are delicious grilled and served as a starter, dressed with hazelnut vinaigrette and a scattering of Västerbotten cheese crumbs.

1 Preheat the grill or barbecue. Gently melt 4 tbsp of the butter (you don't want it to start turning brown, or it will taste burnt). Clarify it by sieving through a paper coffee filter, and then mix with the balsamic vinegar.

2 Stir the hazelnuts into the butter and vinegar mixture. Whizz the bread, cheese and 2 tbsp butter in a food processor to a crumble, then fry in a frying pan on a medium heat until crisp and golden.

3 Snap off the dry, hard bottoms of the asparagus spears. Brush with 1 tbsp melted butter and grill for a couple of minutes each side, or until they have softened slightly but still have some springiness.

4 Divide the asparagus between four plates. Drizzle over the hazelnut dressing, sprinkle with the Västerbotten crumbs and season to taste.

Kycklingspett
CHICKEN KEBABS

4 chicken breasts

8 mushrooms

1 leek

1 bell pepper

8 small tomatoes

4 tbsp oil

1 tsp soy sauce

salt and freshly ground
black pepper

2 tbsp honey

TO SERVE

Potato and Fennel Salad
(see page 116)

SERVES 4

In our family we have the barbecue going in all seasons, and the neighbours presumably think we're completely mad when they see us putting up the parasol against autumn rain and winter snow. It's Pelle, my husband, who is often found firing it up, and he has an instinctive feeling for when the chicken in this recipe is exactly done, but not dry. (Though do note, chicken must always be cooked through!)

1 Preheat the barbecue or grill to a medium heat. Soak 8 wooden skewers to prevent them from burning.

2 Chop the chicken into bite-sized pieces. Clean the mushrooms and slice the leek into 8 pieces. Core the pepper and chop into evenly-sized pieces that will fit on the skewer.

3 Alternate chicken, mushroom, leek, pepper and tomato on each skewer. Mix the oil and soy sauce together and season to taste. Brush the kebabs with the oil mix.

4 Grill the kebabs for 15–20 minutes, turning occasionally, until the juices run clear when you cut into a piece of chicken. Arrange the kebabs on a plate, drizzle the honey over and serve.

Smörgåsbord

The Swedish word *smörgåsbord* is one of the few modern Swedish words to have been taken on by other languages, such as English and German. A *smörgåsbord* is a traditional Swedish buffet that offers a little bit of everything, and guests can take what they like. The dishes vary a little according to season, but herring in all its forms is one of the cornerstones, as are salmon, meatballs and substantial gratins. It isn't unusual to find 50 or 60 dishes on a restaurant *smörgåsbord*, and they tend to contain little in the way of salads, instead focussing on protein. Come Christmas, the *smörgåsbord* takes on its most substantial form, and is rounded off with a hearty rice pudding and a few passes of the *gottebord*, or sweetie table, before guests are allowed to stagger home.

Swedish sandwiches

Scandinavian sandwiches are always open sandwiches with toppings of all kinds piled high, so strictly speaking they are not sandwiches at all! While it's usual to have a sandwich for lunch in other countries, Swedes would usually have their savoury *smörgås* with ham or cheese at breakfast. It's also traditional to have these open sandwiches as a starter, in a smaller version and with more luxurious toppings, and then they are often called by their anglicised name *sandvikare*. My mother used to make three little *sandvikare* as a starter and combine the flavours quite carefully. I think she was inspired by the Danish *smørrebrød* we ate on our trips to Copenhagen.

Sandvikare med rökt ren

SMOKED REINDEER OPEN SANDWICHES WITH HORSERADISH CREAM

8 small slices of sour dough
bread or 4 large slices, halved
(see page 59)

butter, to butter the bread

8 thin slices of smoked reindeer
or other smoked game

100 ml (3½ fl oz) crème fraîche

2 tbsp freshly grated horseradish

few sprigs of fresh parsley

freshly ground black pepper

MAKES 8

Reindeer meat is eaten readily throughout Sweden and reindeer are kept as livestock like any other animal. To us Swedes it isn't any stranger to eat reindeer than it is to eat lamb or beef. This classic combination of smoked reindeer and horseradish is simply delicious. If you cannot get hold of smoked reindeer, it works just as well with any other smoked game.

The Smoked Reindeer Sandwich is photographed opposite accompanied by a Sandwich with Chopped Egg (see page 86) and a Cheese Sandwich (see page 87). These three sandwiches are great served as a starter with a beer and a glass of schnapps (see pages 140–141) – which always gets the dinner party off to a good start!

1 Butter the bread. Roll rosettes from the sliced meat and place one on each slice of bread.

2 Mix the crème fraîche with most of the horseradish, reserving a little for decoration. Spoon a dollop of the horseradish cream onto each sandwich.

3 Sprinkle the reserved horseradish over the sandwiches and garnish with the parsley. Season to taste.

Sandvikare med gubbaröra

SANDWICHES WITH CHOPPED EGG

2 tbsp butter

1 onion, sliced

4 eggs, hard boiled

2 x 125 g (4½ oz) tins Swedish ansjovis (see page 44)

3 tbsp double cream

salt and freshly ground black pepper

8 slices Swedish kavring, or other dark rye bread

chives, to garnish

MAKES 8

Despite being called *gubbaröra* – old man's mishmash in English – and supposedly just the thing for an all-male party after slightly too much alcohol, I have to admit I love this dish. It's a classic at student gatherings such as spring balls, when a bite of something salty is needed in the small hours.

1 Melt the butter in a saucepan and sweat the onion until translucent. Remove from the heat.

2 Peel and chop the eggs. Drain the ansjovis and chop. Carefully fold the chopped fish, egg and cream into the onion. Season to taste.

3 Spread the bread with the fish mix and garnish with the chives.

Sandvikare med ost

CHEESE SANDWICHES

8 slices white bread

butter, to butter the bread

8 small slices of Västerbotten or mature Cheddar cheese

8 small slices Kvibille or Danish blue cheese

2 tbsp quince jelly or Rhubarb Jam (see page 101)

MAKES 8

The third cornerstone in my mother's sandwich selection was always this cheese sandwich. Choose Swedish cheese if possible, but you can swap for something of a similar character, such as a mature Cheddar, if you cannot get hold of it.

1 Cut out a heart shape from each slice of bread – I find it easiest to use a biscuit cutter.

2 Butter the bread and top each heart with slices of Västerbotten and Kvibille cheese.

3 Spoon a little quince jelly or rhubarb jam on top and serve.

Skagenröra

SWEDISH PRAWN COCKTAIL

500 g (1¼ lb) cooked, unpeeled
prawns

6 tbsp mayonnaise

6 tbsp crème fraîche

½ bunch fresh dill

juice and zest of 1 lemon

salt and freshly ground
black pepper

½ tsp brandy (optional)

TO SERVE

thin slices of toasted bread
or baked potatoes

lemon wedges

SERVES 4

I like to use crème fraîche as well as mayonnaise in my version of
this classic dish as it makes for a cleaner, sharper taste. Serve with
toasted bread as a beautiful starter, or in a baked potato as an
excellent lunch. If you fancy some added luxury, try a big dollop
of *kalix löjrom* (vendace roe) on top.

1 Peel the prawns. Set aside a few to use as a garnish and chop
the remainder coarsely.

2 Mix the mayonnaise and crème fraîche together and stir in the
chopped prawns.

3 Set aside a few fronds of dill to use as a garnish and chop the
rest finely. Add the chopped dill to the prawn mixture. Add the
lemon zest and juice to taste – I like to use half a teaspoon of of
zest and one teaspoon of juice – then season and add the brandy,
if using.

4 Serve on thin slices of toasted bread or in a baked potato. Top
with a few whole prawns, a sprinkle of dill and a wedge of lemon.

Gratäng på hälleflundra

MY MOTHER'S HALIBUT AU GRATIN

600 g (1½ lb) halibut fillets

10 mushrooms, sliced

1 whole lobster

3 tbsp butter plus extra
for greasing

3 tbsp plain flour

300 ml (½ pint) double cream

50 ml (2 fl oz) dry white wine

salt and freshly ground
pepper to taste

50 g (2 oz) grated cheese

3 tbsp fine breadcrumbs

2 sprigs of dill

TO SERVE

lemon wedges and freshly baked
Rose Rolls (see opposite)

SERVES 4

Meticulous though she was, sadly my mother never wrote down all of her very best recipes. She made a fish gratin from the most wonderful ingredients – halibut and lobster. Sometimes she served this dish as a starter, but it's so rich I prefer to serve it as a luxurious main course with freshly baked Rose Rolls (see opposite).

1 Preheat the oven to 200°C/400°F/gas 6. Arrange the halibut in the bottom of a large greased ovenproof dish. Place the mushroom slices on top of the fish.

2 Dress the lobster, reserving the meat from the claws for decoration. Scatter the lobster meat over the mushrooms.

3 To make the sauce, melt the butter in a saucepan and whisk in the flour. Add the cream and wine and whisk well. Simmer for 5 minutes, stirring continuously. Season to taste.

4 Pour the sauce over the fish. Mix the cheese and breadcrumbs together and sprinkle on top of the gratin, then bake in the lower part of the oven for 30 minutes.

5 Decorate with the lobster claw meat and dill, and serve immediately with lemon wedges and freshly baked rolls.

Rosenbröd

ROSE ROLLS

50 g (2 oz) fresh baker's yeast

2 tbsp butter

500 ml (18 fl oz) milk

1 tsp salt

approximately 1.25 kg
(2½ lb) plain flour

1 egg, beaten

1 tbsp poppy seeds

MAKES 30

These pretty bread rolls take their name from the way they open up like roses in bloom as they're baked. My mother often served them with a light main course, or as something a bit more substantial to go with a cup of coffee. They are also perfect as part of a buffet.

1 Crumble the yeast into a large mixing bowl. Melt the butter in the milk over a gentle heat and warm to body temperature. Pour the liquid ingredients over the yeast and stir to dissolve.

2 Add the salt and as much flour as needed to make a soft, springy dough. Knead the dough until shiny and smooth, and leave to rise at room temperature in a draught-free place for about 30 minutes.

3 Knock back the dough and knead until smooth. Divide into three equal pieces, roll each out into a long sausage, and divide each into 10 pieces. Roll each piece into a round roll and place on a baking sheet lined with baking parchment. Leave to prove for about 20 minutes. Meanwhile preheat the oven to 250°C/475°F/gas 9.

4 Cut a cross in the top of each of the rolls. Brush each with the beaten egg and sprinkle with poppy seeds. Bake in the middle of the oven for about 10 minutes until the rolls are golden brown and sound hollow when tapped on the bottom. Leave to cool on cooling rack.

Kokt gädda med pepparrot
POACHED PIKE WITH HORSERADISH

1 whole pike weighing about 1.5 kg (3 lb), or 800 g (1¾ lb) fillets

½ onion, chopped

4 sprigs of dill

½ tbsp salt per litre of water used to poach the fish

juice of ½ a lemon

75 g (3 oz) butter

4 cm (1½ in) piece of fresh horseradish, peeled and grated

TO SERVE

boiled potatoes, carrots and mangetout

SERVES 4

My husband grew up in a house in a wonderful lakeside location, on Sövdesjön in Skåne. It's thanks to him that I've learned to appreciate freshwater fish, as I used to be more at home with sea fish. The best thing to do with pike is to poach it and serve it with freshly grated horseradish and melted butter. Your luck's in if it's the season for new potatoes, otherwise regular potatoes will have to do. If you can't get hold of pike, or you don't like it, this recipe works very well with any firm white fish.

1 Gut and scale the fish, or wipe the fish fillets clean. Place in a large saucepan or deep frying pan and cover with cold water so that it just covers the fish.

2 Add the onion to the saucepan along with the dill, salt and lemon juice. Bring the fish to a simmer over a medium heat and cook very gently for around 10 minutes until the flesh is white and just coming away from the bones.

3 Meanwhile gently melt the butter. You don't want it to turn brown otherwise it will taste burnt. Remove the fish from the pan carefully so that it doesn't fall apart, and serve on a large fish dish or divided between warmed plates. Top with the grated horseradish, drizzle with melted butter and serve with boiled potatoes, carrots and mangetout.

Fläskpannkaka

SWEDISH TOAD IN THE HOLE

180 g (6½ oz) plain flour

pinch of salt

600 ml (1 pint) milk

3 eggs

3 tbsp butter

300 g (11 oz) smoked bacon

TO SERVE

Lingonberry Jam (see page 176) and grated raw carrot

SERVES 4

My daughter Sara is to thank for this comforting dish. She first made this when she wanted to show our Italian exchange student a typical everyday Swedish meal, and this seemed the best way to demonstrate simple home cooking. If you are used to toad in the hole made with sausages, it may surprise you to see that the Swedish version is made with smoked bacon instead. But trust me, this version is quick to cook and delicious, especially when served with Lingonberry Jam (see page 176) and grated raw carrot.

1 Preheat the oven to 225°C/425°F/gas 7. Put the flour and salt into a mixing bowl. Add the milk a little at a time, whisking after each addition. Beat in the eggs. Finally melt the butter and whisk into the batter.

2 Cube the bacon and scatter in the bottom of a large, greased ovenproof dish. Bake in the oven for 5 minutes. Pour the batter into the dish and bake for a further 20 minutes, until it's set and golden brown.

3 Serve immediately with Lingonberry Sauce and grated raw carrot.

Lammfärsjärpar med fårostsås

LAMB CROQUETTES WITH CHEESE SAUCE

2 tbsp breadcrumbs

3 tbsp cold water

½ red onion, finely grated

600 g (1½ lb) lamb mince

1 egg, beaten

salt and freshly ground
black pepper

FOR THE SAUCE

100 g (4 oz) ewe's milk cheese

300 ml (½ pint) crème fraîche

½ tbsp fresh rosemary,
stripped from the stalk

salt and freshly ground
black pepper

TO SERVE

potato wedges and a crisp,
green salad

SERVES 4

Sheep farming is common in southern Sweden, out in the beautiful region of Österlen, and I usually try to buy lamb mince direct from the farm. If you're really lucky, you'll find farmers who produce their own ewe's milk cheese, otherwise you should be able to find this ingredient in your local supermarket.

1 Mix the breadcrumbs and water together in a mixing bowl and leave for 5 minutes so the bread absorbs the water. Add the onion, lamb mince and the beaten egg. Season with salt and pepper.

2 Mix until smooth using a wooden spoon or your hands. Shape tablespoonfuls of meat into oval croquettes and shallow fry in butter until golden.

3 To make the sauce, crumble the cheese into a small saucepan and mix in the crème fraîche and rosemary. Bring to a simmer, remove from the heat and season.

4 Serve the croquettes with the sauce, potato wedges and a green salad.

Rabarberpaj

RHUBARB CRUMBLE

700 g (1½ lb) rhubarb,
peeled and sliced

4 tbsp caster sugar

2 tbsp potato flour or
cornflour

90 g (3½ oz) plain flour

60 g (2½ oz) rolled oats

75 g (3 oz) butter

SERVES 4–6

In early spring the first rhubarb buds appear in my garden
and it's not long before the stems are long enough to harvest for
a wonderful crumble. This is perfect with custard, whipped cream
or ice cream, and can be eaten both as a cake with coffee or as
a dessert.

1 Preheat the oven to 225°C/425°F/gas 7. Grease a medium
ovenproof dish. Place the rhubarb in the dish, sprinkle with
3 tbsp of the sugar and the potato flour or cornflour.

2 Mix the plain flour, oats and the remaining sugar together in
a mixing bowl. Rub in the butter into the dry ingredients to make
a crumble.

3 Spread the crumble over the rhubarb and bake in the centre
of the oven for about 20 minutes until the top is golden brown.

Rabarber under nötmaräng

RHUBARB WITH HAZELNUT MERINGUE TOPPING

600 g (1½ lb) rhubarb, peeled and sliced

80 g (3½ oz) golden caster sugar, plus 3 tbsp

½ tsp vanilla sugar

2 tsp potato flour or cornflour

75 g (3 oz) hazelnuts

2 egg whites

TO SERVE

vanilla ice cream

SERVES 4

The acidity of the rhubarb combined with the sweetness of the meringue creates a wonderful flavour. This dessert is so easy to make, but gives the impression of being rather luxurious. That's my kind of cookery!

1 Preheat the oven to 175°C/350°F/gas 4. Grease four ovenproof ramekins and divide the rhubarb between them. Sprinkle over 80 g (3½ oz) caster sugar, the vanilla sugar and the potato flour or cornflour. Bake in the centre of the oven for 10 minutes. Meanwhile whiz the hazelnuts in a food processor until finely chopped but not oily.

2 Beat the egg whites until they form soft peaks. Whisk in 3 tbsp caster sugar and then carefully fold in the chopped nuts without knocking the air out of the meringue. Remove the ramekins from the oven and raise the temperature to 225°C/425°/gas 7.

3 Spread the meringue over the rhubarb and bake at the bottom of the oven for about 5 minutes, until the meringue is slightly set and golden. Serve warm with vanilla ice cream.

Rabarbermarmelad

RHUBARB JAM

1 kg (2 lb) rhubarb, peeled
and thinly sliced

juice of 1 lemon

1 tbsp ground ginger

750 g (1½ lb) granulated sugar

**MAKES APPROXIMATELY
1 KG (2 LB)**

Homemade jam for breakfast is a real treat. This jam is also terrifically good with a piece of mature cheese – try it with the Cheese Sandwiches on page 87. The tartness of the rhubarb works extremely well with the ginger.

1 Place the rhubarb in a large saucepan or preserving pan. Add the lemon juice, ginger and sugar and leave to stand in a cool place for several hours, or preferably overnight.

2 Place the uncovered pan on a medium heat and gently bring to a simmer. Cook for about 45 minutes until it reaches a jammy consistency, stirring occasionally so that it doesn't burn.

3 Pour into sterilized jars and seal.

Sockerkaka

SPONGE CAKE

300 g (11 oz) eggs, weighed
in their shells

300 g (11 oz) caster sugar

150 g (5 oz) plain flour

TO SERVE

whipped cream and
fresh berries

My mother often baked sponge cakes when I was a child. When my daughter Sara was little, she used to take slices of sponge cake home from granny's to keep in the freezer, ready for her to enjoy whenever she felt like it. A real treat!

What makes this sponge cake so fantastic is that it is almost like a meringue on top and is actually pretty squidgy for a sponge cake. To make it extra special cut it in half and sandwich with fresh berries and whipped cream, then decorate with more berries.

1 Preheat the oven to 175°C/350°F/gas 4. Beat the eggs and sugar together until thick and pale. Carefully fold in the flour without knocking the air out of the mixture.

2 Pour into a greased and floured 20 cm (8 in) springform cake tin. Bake at the bottom of the oven for about 35 minutes. If a skewer inserted into the middle of the cake comes out clean, then the cake is ready.

3 Turn the cake out immediately and leave to cool on a cooling rack. Serve with whipped cream and fresh berries.

Chokladrulltårta

CHOCOLATE ROLL

3 eggs

165 g (5½ oz) caster sugar, plus extra for sprinkling over the finished cake

75 g (3 oz) potato flour or cornflour

1 tbsp plain flour

2 tbsp cocoa powder

½ tsp vanilla sugar

1 tsp baking powder

FILLING

150 g (5 oz) softened butter

2 egg yolks

110 g (4½ oz) caster sugar

½ tsp vanilla sugar

SERVES 8-10

When I worked as a domestic science teacher I always taught my classes how to a bake this chocolate roll. It can be whisked together in no time, and only takes 5 minutes to bake. This is perfect with a cup of coffee when you have an unexpected visitor, or anytime you are in the mood for a bit of cake!

1 Preheat the oven to 250°C/475°F/gas 9. Line a large shallow roasting tin with baking parchment and fold up the corners, or use a Swiss roll tin. Beat the eggs and sugar together until thick and pale.

2 Mix the flours, cocoa, vanilla sugar and baking powder together in a mixing bowl, then fold carefully into the egg mix. Spread the cake mix onto the baking parchment and bake in the oven for 5 minutes.

3 Turn the cake out of the tin, dampening the baking parchment a little if it won't peel off. Sprinkle a little sugar over the cake and leave to cool on a cooling rack.

4 Whisk the ingredients for the filling together and spread over the cake. Roll the cake up from the long side to form a 'roll' shape. Slice and serve.

Våfflor

WAFFLES

100 g (4 oz) butter

400 ml (14 fl oz) milk

1 tsp baking powder

180 g (6¼ oz) plain flour

TO SERVE

fresh berries or jam

whipped cream or vanilla
ice cream

MAKES 6–8

In Sweden, it's traditional to eat waffles for Annunciation, or Lady Day as it's also known, on 25 March. One memorable holiday, my father, who never cooked, decided to surprise us by making waffles for everyone. It all finished with him impugning my mother's lovely old waffle iron, saying that it made everything stick – even though it had worked perfectly for at least 30 years! I can promise you that they're really not that difficult to make…

1 Melt the butter but don't let it brown, and set it aside to cool slightly.

2 Mix half the milk with the baking powder and flour to form a smooth batter. Add the remaining milk and cooled butter.

3 Heat your waffle iron and brush with butter, if needed. Pour in 75 ml (2¾ fl oz) of the batter at a time, and cook the waffles until golden.

4 Serve immediately with fresh berries or jam, and whipped cream or vanilla ice cream.

Kringlor

JUMBLES

200 g (7 oz) butter

200 g (7 oz) plain flour

50 ml (2 fl oz) cold water

110 g (4¼ oz) caster sugar,
plus extra for dipping

MAKES ABOUT 60

In old Swedish films and books, especially in Astrid Lindgren's books, there is always a sign in the shape of a jumble hanging over the town's bakery. There certainly was in the little town where I grew up, and at school we used to sing a children's song about the town confectioner. These old-fashioned jumbles are the Swedish answer to Italian *biscotti*, and I often bake a batch to take along to meetings at work. Perfect with a caffè latte.

1 Combine all of the ingredients and leave to rest in the fridge for around 30 minutes. Meanwhile preheat the oven to 200°C/400°F/gas 6.

2 Divide the dough into two equal parts and shape into long rolls. Cut each roll into 30 equal pieces.

3 Roll each piece into a long sausage and twist. Dip in caster sugar. Place on a baking sheet lined with baking parchment and bake in the centre of the oven for 8 minutes.

4 Leave to cool on a cooling rack. The jumbles will keep in an airtight container for a week or so, or they can be frozen – they only take a few minutes to thaw.

Kladdkaka

CHOCOLATE STICKY CAKE

100 g (4 oz) dark chocolate
(minimum 70% cocoa)

100 g (4 oz) butter

2 eggs

165 g (5½ oz) caster sugar

90 g (3½ oz) plain flour

1 tsp vanilla sugar

1 tsp baking powder

TO SERVE
whipped cream, crème
fraîche or thick yoghurt

SERVES 8

I never tire of this deliciously sticky chocolate cake, and it always surprises me that something so simple to make can be so amazingly good to eat. Be sure to use good quality chocolate in this recipe, as it really does make all the difference.

1 Preheat the oven to 175°C/350°F/gas 4. Grease and line a 25 cm (10 in) cake tin. Roughly chop the chocolate, reserving a little for decoration. Melt the chopped chocolate with the butter in a bowl over a pan of barely simmering water then set aside to cool slightly.

2 Beat the eggs and sugar together. In a seperate bowl combine the flour, vanilla sugar and baking powder.

3 Fold the melted chocolate and butter into the egg mixture, then fold in the dry ingredients until smooth. Pour into the cake tin and bake in the centre of the oven for 15–20 minutes, until the cake is cooked through at the edges but still sticky in the middle.

4 Leave the cake in the tin to cool thoroughly – the chocolate in the cake needs time to set before it can be cut. Meanwhile grate the reserved chocolate.

5 Remove the cake from the tin and decorate with the grated chocolate. Serve with whipped cream, crème fraîche or thick yoghurt.

Kladdkaka   8 bitar

100 g choklad
100 g smör
2 ägg
1,5 dl strösocker
1,5 dl vetemjöl
1 tsk vaniljsocker
1 krm bakpulver

Hacka chokladen, smält med smör
Vispa ägg och socker. Blanda
samman alla torra ingredienser.

Rör samman choklad- & äggsmet,
och torrvarorna, till en klumpfri
smet.

Häll i smord, bröad rund form
och grädda 15-20 minuter.
Låt stelna & svalna.

Summer
SOMMAR

Summer in Sweden

Swedish summers tend to be short, which is why we Swedes throw ourselves into summer activities and holidays. Many people are known to take four weeks off work and head out to a summer cottage in the countryside. Given that the snow doesn't melt until June in the north of Sweden, and will start falling again in October, it's not surprising everyone wants to make the most of the warmth and the light. I went to university in Umeå up in Norrland, the most northerly part of Sweden, and having experienced the winters there I now really appreciate the longer summers far south in Skåne. It has to be pouring with rain and blowing a gale before Swedes will admit defeat and celebrate Midsummer Eve indoors, and the joke goes that it's only when the schnapps is being diluted by the rain that it's time to go back inside.

If there is one taste that makes a Swedish summer for me, it has to be dill. This straggly, dull-looking herb rises to kitchen stardom when the time comes for summer food. While Swedes use dill all year round, home-grown dill is ready to be picked at about the same time as the first new potatoes are lifted. Potatoes are almost always cooked with a few sprigs of dill, and then garnished with a dusting of finely chopped dill just before serving. Dill is used in many light summer sauces to go with fish, and in many pickles, too. Later, when autumn begins to creep in at the end of August and it's time for a crayfish party, the dill will have grown tall and produced its 'crowns' of seeds. Crayfish are cooked with great fistfuls of the herb and then decorated with the beautiful heads.

Summer is, of course, berry season. First strawberries, then currants, raspberries, gooseberries and bilberries follow in perfect succession. In the summer I eat berries in some form nearly every day, often just as they are. The most luxurious of all are probably sun-warmed wild strawberries, threaded on a long blade of grass to take with us to the beach. This profusion of berries also stirs a gatherer instinct, as it's the time to make jam and fruit syrups ready to be enjoyed in the long cold winter. We Swedes pick punnets and punnets of strawberries at pick-your-own farms, and make enough jam to last until the following summer – just perfect with pancakes, waffles, rice pudding or scones.

Grillrökt lax

BARBECUE SMOKED SALMON

800 g (1¾ lb) salmon fillet, skin-on

2 tsp salt flakes

2 tbsp rapeseed oil

3 tbsp mustard

2 tbsp honey

3 tbsp chopped herbs, such as tarragon, parsley and basil

2 tbsp breadcrumbs

TO SERVE

Potato and Fennel Salad (see page 116)

SERVES 4

The secret to the smoky taste of this delicious salmon dish is to add wood to the charcoal and close the lid of the barbeque. Any kind of wood will do, as long as it is untreated, and we usually lop a few small branches off our apple tree to use. Once the barbecue is lit we clap on the lid and let the smoke build up before slipping the salmon onto the grate and leaving it to hot smoke. This always goes down a storm at summer parties, and is particularly good when served with the Potato and Fennel Salad on page 116.

1 Soak the pieces of wood in water for an hour or so, then light the barbecue. Just before you are ready to cook, put the wood chips on top of the fuel, close the lid and let the smoke build up.

2 Salt the salmon and place skin side down on a piece of foil slightly larger than the fish. Mix the remaining ingredients together and spread over on the salmon.

3 Cook the salmon on a grate as high above the heat as possible, with the lid on, for around 10 minutes until just cooked. Serve with a potato and fennel salad.

Potatis- och fänkålssallad

POTATO AND FENNEL SALAD

1 kg (2 lb) new potatoes

1 head of fennel, finely sliced

2 spring onions, finely sliced

1 orange bell pepper, finely sliced

100 ml (3 ½ fl oz) lemon juice

75 ml (2½ fl oz) good olive oil

salt and freshly ground
black pepper

SERVES 4

This potato salad is perfect as part of a buffet or to accompany grilled meats or fish at a barbecue. Simplicity itself to prepare, and ready well in advance, all you have to do is put it on the table when the guests arrive. I prefer potato salads with a vinaigrette or citronette dressing to mayonnaise dressings, which I find can be greasy. My variation, made with crisp fennel, goes well with fish dishes such as the Barbecue Smoked Salmon on page 115, and also with chicken.

1 Scrub the potatoes and boil them in lightly salted water until just cooked. Leave to cool, then slice.

2 Mix the vegetables together in large salad bowl. Whisk together the lemon juice and oil, and season to taste.

3 Pour the dressing over the salad and leave to stand for a couple of hours before serving.

Västerbottenflarn

VÄSTERBOTTEN CHEESE LACE BISCUITS

200 g (7 oz) Västerbotten cheese (or any hard, mature cheese), finely grated

16 Kalamata olives, stoned and sliced

SERVES 4 AS A NIBBLE

Rather than preparing a starter when I have friends over for dinner, I like to arrange a few nibbles to go with a glass of wine for them to enjoy while I put the finishing touches to the meal, and these lace biscuits are just the thing. I still haven't managed to make enough for there to be any left over, as they really do vanish at quite a speed! If you do ever manage to have any left, they are super as a garnish for a salad or fish.

Västerbotten cheese is outstanding to cook with and works well as a substitute for Parmesan, just as these biscuits will still be delicious if you use Parmesan in this recipe.

1 Preheat the oven to 200°C/400°F/gas 6. Line a baking sheet with baking parchment.

2 Spoon small heaps of the cheese onto the lined baking sheet, leaving space in between as the cheese will spread as it melts. Place an olive slice onto each cheese heap.

3 Bake in the centre of the oven for about 5 minutes, or until golden brown and melted. Leave to cool on a cooling rack.

Spickeskinka snacks

HAM JERKY

200 g (7 oz) best quality
salt cured smoked
ham, sliced

SERVES 4 AS A NIBBLE

These easy-to-make snacks are a tasty alternative to ready-made crisps. I like to pass these round with a glass of wine when guests arrive for a dinner or drinks party. If you have any left over, ham jerky is delicious added to a pasta salad. Choose a good, locally-produced ham for the best results – the taste is concentrated as the meat dries in the oven so it really is worth going for the best ham you can find.

1 Preheat the oven to 175°C/350°/gas 4. Place the slices of ham on a baking sheet lined with baking parchment. Cook in the centre of the oven for 3–5 minutes until the fat has melted away and the slices are beginning to brown (although make sure they don't burn).

2 Leave to go cold – the jerky will harden as it cools. Break into bite-sized pieces and serve.

Grillade morötter

BARBECUED CARROTS

1 bunch of early carrots,
scrubbed clean

3 tbsp butter

1 tbsp fresh herbs of your choice

1 tsp sea salt

100 ml (3½ fl oz) dry white wine

SERVES 4

Summer carrots are lovely, and when they're at their most tender they don't even need peeling. They are an excellent accompaniment for almost anything from the barbecue, and it's handy to cook all the food outside rather than have to trot backwards and forwards to the kitchen.

1 Preheat the barbecue or grill. Place the carrots a sheet of foil. Dot with the butter and sprinkle over the herbs and salt.

2 Fold up the edges of the foil up and pour over the wine. Fold the foil to seal well, then place on the barbecue (or under the grill) where it isn't too hot. The cooking time depends on the size of the carrots but it will probably be around 15–20 minutes.

3 Remove the foil package from the barbecue or grill and place the carrots to a serving dish. Pour over the cooking juices and serve.

Rostade rödbetor med fetaostkräm

BAKED BEETROOT WITH FETA CREAM

1 kg (2 lb) fresh beetroot, peeled
and cut into wedges

2 tbsp butter

1 tsp sea salt

200 g (7 oz) feta cheese

200 ml (⅓ pint) crème fraîche

1 tsp fresh rosemary

SERVES 4

The combination of beetroot and feta cheese is just sublime, and what could be easier than roasting fresh beetroot and simply topping with a dollop of feta cream. This is a fantastic accompaniment for meat or fish and is ideal to serve as part of a buffet or as a starter.

1 Preheat the oven to 200°C/400°F/gas 6. Place the beetroot wedges into a greased ovenproof dish and sprinkle with the salt.

2 Bake for about 15 minutes in the centre of the oven until the beetroot has begun to soften. Meanwhile whizz the feta cheese and the crème fraîche in a food processor.

3 Remove the beetroot from the oven and sprinkle with rosemary. Spoon over the feta cream and bake for a further 10 minutes.

Primörsallad

PRIMEUR SALAD

8–10 new potatoes, scrubbed

4 spring onions

8 radishes

200 g (7 oz) mangetout

DRESSING

50 ml (2 fl oz) rapeseed oil

2 tbsp white wine vinegar

2 tbsp sweetish mustard

1 tsp fresh thyme

salt and freshly ground
black pepper

SERVES 4

After a long winter with masses of root vegetables, the Swedish early vegetables are much anticipated. I love the early summer harvest, particularly mild spring onions, radishes before they become too peppery, mangetout peas, and, last but not least, new potatoes. This salad is delicious with smoked mackerel.

1 Halve any large potatoes and boil in lightly salted water. Add the spring onions, radishes and mangetout peas for a couple of minutes at the end of the cooking time. Drain and leave the vegetables to steam dry and cool.

2 Arrange the vegetables in a serving bowl. Whisk together the ingredients for the dressing. Pour the dressing over the vegetables and serve the salad lukewarm or cold.

Fläderblomssaft

ELDERFLOWER CORDIAL

2 kg (4½ lb) granulated sugar

3 tsp citric acid

30 heads of elderflower
in full bloom

4 lemons, sliced

**MAKES 2.5–3 LITRES
(4½–5½ PINTS**

Ever since my daughter Sara was little we've picked elderflowers
to make cordial. Here in southern Sweden the flowers are ready
around Midsummer, or just before, and it's quick work to pick
them. After the flowers have sat in the syrup for a few days
you'll have a fragrant, refreshing cordial to enjoy on a hot
summer's afternoon.

Elderflower cordial is the perfect base for a delicious
welcoming drink for a summer party. Mix the cordial with
sparkling white wine and add a few fresh berries to the glass.

1 Pour 1.5 litres (2½ pints) cold water into a large saucepan.
Bring to the boil and stir in the sugar and citric acid.

2 Place the flower heads and the lemon slices into a very large
bowl or clean bucket. Pour the hot sugary water into the bowl or
bucket and leave to cool. Cover and leave in a cool place for
3–4 days, stirring frequently.

3 Drain the cordial through a fine sieve or jelly strainer. Pour
into sterilized bottles or jars and store in the fridge. (To store for
longer than a week, freeze the cordial in a suitable container.)

Rårörd jordgubbssaft

RAW STRAWBERRY CORDIAL

2 kg (4½ lb) strawberries, rinsed
and hulled

1 litre (1¾ pints) cold water

3 tsp citric acid

2 kg (4½ lb) caster sugar

**MAKES ABOUT 2 LITRES
(3½ PINTS)**

Take the opportinuty to make this cordial when strawberries are at their best and cheapest. Since this cordial isn't cooked, it has a wonderful taste but a shorter shelf life. If you have the space, freeze it in plastic pots instead, and all winter you can enjoy homemade cordial without a long list of additives.

1 Purée the strawberries with the water in a food processor and add the citric acid. Leave to stand for 48 hours in the fridge, then drain through a fine sieve or jelly strainer.

2 Add the sugar and stir until it has dissolved completely. Pour into sterilized bottles or jars and store in the fridge. (To store for longer than a week, freeze the cordial in a suitable container.)

Party time

The summer solstice has been celebrated for thousands of years, and it is known that our ancestors arranged festivities to honour the longest day of the year. The Christian Church then linked the celebration of Midsummer with a Christian holiday when, in the fourth century, the 24th of June was named as the Feast of St John the Baptist (in Luke it's said that John the Baptist was born six months before Jesus). Ever since, the Church in Sweden has fought a losing battle to ensure the celebrations are Christian rather than heathen. At a Swedish Midsummer celebration we dance around a leafy maypole, and eat pickled herring and new potatoes followed by the first strawberries of the season. Schnapps is another must. As of 1954, Swedish Midsummer is celebrated on the Friday between 19 and 25 June, and so not always on the day of the actual summer solstice.

My Midsummer

Midsummer is my favourite time of year. I love the greenness, the flowers and the magically light evenings. Some Midsummers it's all about the herring – umpteen kinds of pickled herring and mattie herring with sour cream and chives – so wonderful served simply with a steaming bowl of new potatoes and followed by freshly picked strawberries. Other years I prepare morsels of Mattie Herring on Crispbread (see page 134) as appetizers, perhaps with a Mattie Herring Tart (see page 74), and then Barbecue Smoked Salmon (see page 115) with Potato and Fennel Salad (see page 116) for the main course, after which there's no better finish than a Strawberry Gateau (see page 154) for dessert.

Matjessill på knäckebröd

MATTIE HERRING ON CRISPBREAD

4–6 small new potatoes

1 x 200 g (7 oz) jar of mattie herring (see page 73)

8–12 small crispbreads

100 ml (3½ fl oz) sour cream

10 chives, finely chopped

SERVES 4

Herring, potatoes, sour cream and chives are what Midsummer is all about, and so I like to serve canapés of herring on crispbread as a starter, and then enjoy a barbecue. Mattie herring can be bought from specialist Swedish food shops (see Stockists on page 219).

1 Boil the potatoes in lightly salted water until just cooked. Leave to cool, then slice thinly. Drain the mattie herring and cut into bite-sized pieces.

2 Butter the crispbreads. Top each with a slice of potato and some herring. Spoon on a little sour cream and sprinkle with chives. Serve immediately so the crispbread doesn't go soggy.

Nypotatis med löjrom

NEW POTATOES WITH VENDACE ROE

16 small new potatoes

100 ml (3½ fl oz) crème fraîche

50 g (2 oz) vendace or lumpfish roe

6 chives, sliced

SERVES 4

I like to serve these little morsels as an appetiser with a glass of wine while my guests wait for the meal, often something from the barbecue at this time of year. This dish is also perfect as part of a buffet, and vendace roe can be swapped for lumpfish roe if you prefer.

1 Boil the potatoes in lightly salted water until just cooked (at all costs avoid over-cooking them). Drain and leave to steam dry.

2 Once the potatoes are cool, cut a cross in the top of each and squeeze gently so the potato opens up.

3 Spoon a small dollop of crème fraîche into each, followed by a spoonful of vendace roe. Garnish with the chives.

Schnapps

As soon as herring or crayfish are on the table, a glass of schnapps is bound to follow. Many Swedish dishes are quite salty so the best drink to accompany them is not wine, but beer with a schnapps on the side. Schnapps is traditionally a bitter-flavoured shot of vodka, served in a tall glass measuring only 6 cl. The most common type of schnapps is aquavit, which gets its distinct flavour from a combination of dill and cumin. Some people prefer a fruity or sweet schnapps, often with flavours of berries, while hardcore schnapps drinkers are likely to go for a bitter taste such as wormwood. It's considered extremely rude to drink schnapps without toasting your fellow guests first, and it's almost impossible to drink a schnapps without singing. Many Swedes know a wide variety of drinking songs by heart. There is a schnapps song for every occasion, whether it is to celebrate a special dish, festival or just the season. So join in and don't forget to say *skål*!

Citronsnaps

LEMON SCHNAPPS

375 ml (13 fl oz) Brännvin
Special, or equivalent
flavourless spirit
(such as vodka)

2 unwaxed lemons

MAKES 400 ML (14 FL OZ)

The few times a year I drink schnapps, I prefer the weaker sort
that I have made myself. This lemon schnapps, with its fresh taste,
is one of my favourites.

1 Decant the alcohol into a bottle large enough to hold 400 ml
(14 fl oz) of liquid.

2 Peel the lemons thinly with a vegetable peeler, avoiding cutting
off the pith at the same time (you can always scrape the pith from
the peel if you have to) as it will give the schnapps a bitter taste.
Push the peel into the bottle and seal.

3 Leave the schnapps to stand for a few days, then taste to see if
it is sufficiently lemony. If you want to boost the flavour, squeeze
lemon juice into the schnapps on the day it is to be drunk.

Svartvinbärssnaps

BLACKCURRANT SCHNAPPS

375 ml (13 fl oz) Brännvin
Special, or equivalent
flavourless spirit
(such as vodka)

300 g (11 oz) fresh blackcurrants

MAKES 400 ML (14 FL OZ)

Blackcurrant schnapps is truly wonderful. Some people prefer a more robust, spiced schnapps or aquavit, but I think one flavoured with blackcurrants works with all types of food.

1 Decant the alcohol into a bottle large enough to hold 400 ml (14 fl oz) of liquid.

2 Pick over and clean the blackberries, then push them into the bottle and seal.

3 Leave to stand for about two weeks, tasting every few days until the desired depth of flavour has been reached. Drain the the schnapps to remove the berries (if the berries are left in they will eventually ferment and so should be taken out).

Ost-och skinkgifflar

CHEESE AND HAM CRESCENTS

50 g (2 oz) butter

500 ml (18 fl oz) water

50 g (2 oz) fresh baker's yeast

200 ml (⅓ pint) *filmjölk* (Swedish soured milk) or 100 ml (3½ fl oz) plain yoghurt mixed with 100 ml (3½ fl oz) milk

½ tsp salt

2 eggs, plus 1 beaten egg to glaze

480 – 540 g (1 – 1¼ lb) plain flour

16 slices smoked ham

16 slices strong cheese

16 slices tomato

MAKES 16

These crescents, with the filling baked-in, are a great alternative to sweaty cheese sandwiches at picnics and are perfect to have in the freezer ready to pop into the picnic basket for a walk in the woods or a day out at the beach. If you put them to thaw on a sun-warmed rock while you tackle the berry bushes they'll taste freshly baked.

1 Melt the butter in a saucepan. Add the water and warm to body temperature. Crumble the yeast into a large mixing bowl and pour over the melted butter and water. Stir until the yeast has dissolved.

2 Add the *filmjölk* (or yoghurt and milk mixture), salt and two eggs, and work in enough flour to form a soft, springy dough. Leave to rise at room temperature for 30 minutes. Knock back the dough and knead until shiny.

3 Divide the dough into two and roll out each half into a large circle, then divide each circle into eight equal pieces. Put a slice of ham, a slice of cheese and a slice of tomato on each piece, and roll up the dough. Place the crescents on a baking sheet and leave to prove for a further 30 minutes.

4 Preheat the oven to 250°C/475°F/gas 9. Brush the crescents with the beaten egg and bake in the middle of the oven for about 10–15 minutes until golden brown.

Tomatsoppa
TOMATO SOUP

1–2 onions, chopped

2 tbsp butter

750 g (1½ lb) very ripe tomatoes,
cored and chopped

1 litre (1¾ pints) vegetable stock

pinch of paprika

salt and freshly ground
black pepper

1½ tbsp plain flour

50 ml (2 fl oz) double cream

2 tbsp sherry

SERVES 4

In late summer, when the greenhouse is collapsing under the weight of tomatoes, there's no way you can eat them all fresh. It is a bit of a shame that they all ripen at the same time, but I take the opportunity to make tomato soup, which I then freeze as a summer memory for a cold winter's day. I like to keep both the skin and the seeds to provide a bit of texture so I don't sieve them out of my soup, but you can remove them if you prefer.

1 Sweat the onions in 1 tbsp of the butter until translucent. Add the tomatoes, stock and paprika and season to taste. Simmer for 10 minutes on a gentle heat.

2 In a seperate saucepan melt the remaining butter and add the flour to form a roux. Whisk this into the soup and simmer for a further 5 minutes. Add the cream and sherry and serve.

Grillade musslor

GRILLED MUSSELS

1 kg (2 lb) fresh mussels

75 g (3 oz) butter

1 clove of garlic

1 tsp chopped fresh herbs, such as parsley, basil, and tarragon

½ tsp sea salt

SERVES 8 AS PART OF A BUFFET

In the late summer, mussel-picking is permitted in some areas on the Swedish west coast and they are delicious cooked simply on a barbecue. Grilled mussels are perfect as part of a buffet, or just as a snack with a slice of bread.

1 Preheat the barbecue or grill. Scrub the mussels well and scrape off the beards. Tap the mussels lightly and throw away any that do not close.

2 Using a spoon, beat the butter in bowl to soften it. Press the garlic into the butter, then mix in the herbs and salt.

3 Put the mussels on the barbecue or under the grill, cover and cook until they have opened, which should take about 3 minutes. Discard any mussels that do not open.

4 Arrange the mussels on a serving dish and spoon over the herb and garlic butter while they are still warm.

Fiskgryta
FISH STEW

6 small onions, chopped

2 tbsp rapeseed oil

4 medium potatoes, peeled
and chopped

2 carrots, peeled
and chopped

1 parsnip, peeled
and chopped

1 small celeriac, peeled
and chopped

400 g (14 oz) can whole tomatoes

100 ml (3½ fl oz) white wine

200 ml (⅓ pint) cold water

3 tbsp concentrated liquid
fish stock

1 bay leaf

400 g (14 oz) fillets of white,
firm-fleshed fish, cut into
bite-sized pieces

zest and juice of 1 lemon

salt and freshly ground
black pepper

½ bunch parsley, chopped

SERVES 4

Fish stew is easy to vary with different sorts of root vegetable and firm-fleshed fish. Simmer the fish on a very gentle heat, otherwise it will fall to pieces and leave the stew looking less appetizing.

1 Fry the onion in the oil until soft. Add the potatoes, carrots, parsnip and celeriac and sizzle for a few minutes.

2 Add the tomatoes, wine, water, concentrated fish stock and bay leaf. Simmer for 10–15 minutes until the vegetables have softened slightly.

3 Put the fish into the stew to cook over a low heat for around 10 minutes until the fish is just firm.

4 Add the lemon zest and juice and season to taste. Sprinkle the parsley over the stew just before serving.

Räkmacka

PRAWN SANDWICHES

1.5 kg (3 lb) cooked,
unpeeled prawns

1 egg yolk

2 tsp lemon juice, plus
zest to taste

salt and freshly ground
black pepper

200 ml (⅓ pint) good olive oil

½ bunch fresh dill, finely chopped

4 slices freshly baked,
good white bread

SERVES 4

Fresh prawns from the fishing village of Smögen on good bread with homemade mayonnaise bring back happy memories of a summer spent along the Swedish west coast and round Danish Zealand. These prawn sandwiches are amazingly good, while sailing as well as on dry land.

1 Peel the prawns, but don't rinse them – instead pick them over to remove any whiskery bits.

2 Break the egg yolk into a bowl, add the lemon juice and season to taste. Whisk for a couple of minutes and then add the oil, drop by drop, whisking continuously. (The mayonnaise will separate if the oil is poured in too quickly, although sometimes it can be rescued by whisking in a few drops of lukewarm water.)

3 Reserve a little of the dill for garnish and mix the remainder into the mayonnaise along with the lemon zest.

4 Butter the bread, pile on the prawns and dollop mayonnaise over the top. Finish with a sprinkling of dill.

Plättbakelser

PANCAKE STACKS WITH BERRIES

125 g (4 oz) plain flour

pinch of salt

300 ml (½ pint) whole milk

2 eggs

25 g (1 oz) butter, plus extra
for frying

TO SERVE

fresh berries sprinkled
with light muscovado sugar

chocolate ice cream

SERVES 4

I have a real weakness for pancake stacks and I like to serve them with seasonal fruits. Most of all I love picking fresh berries in the woods or garden to go with my pancakes and then scooping over chocolate ice cream.

1 Sift the flour into a mixing bowl and add the salt. Pour over half of the milk and whisk until combined. Add the eggs and the remaining milk and whisk again until you have a smooth, lump-free batter.

2 Melt the butter in a medium frying pan and then whisk the melted butter into the pancake batter. Heat a little butter in the pan and drop in 1–2 tablespoon of the batter. Cook for about 30 seconds over a medium heat. Flip the pancake over (or turn using a palette knife) and cook the other side until golden brown. Cook the remaining batter in the same way.

3 Layer the pancakes with berries sprinkled with a little muscovado sugar and spoonfuls of chocolate ice cream.

Hallonglass

RASPBERRY ICE CREAM

250 g (9 oz) frozen raspberries

1 egg

110 g (4¼ oz) golden caster sugar

½ tsp vanilla sugar

100 ml (3½ fl oz) double cream

SERVES 4

This ice cream is quick to make and is a real hit at summer parties. As it contains raw egg be prudent when serving as it may not be suitable for all your guests.

1 Whizz the raspberries to a mush in a food processor. Break in the egg and whizz again until combined.

2 Add both sugars and whizz until well mixed. Finally add the cream in a steady stream until the mixture is creamy and soft.

3 Serve immediately – despite its name, this ice cream isn't really suitable for freezing as it becomes rock hard and full of ice crystals.

Jordgubbscarpaccio

STRAWBERRY CARPACCIO

500 g (1¼ lb) fresh strawberries,
sliced as thinly as possible

4 tbsp white balsamic vinegar

zest of 1 lemon

2 tbsp muscovado sugar

about 12 basil leaves

SERVES 4

I love to eat freshly picked strawberries that have been warmed by the sun, just as they are, and when strawberries are at their best we Swedes eat them like sweets almost every day. This simple carpaccio makes for a light yet elegant dessert.

1 Arrange the strawberry slices on four dessert plates and drizzle each with 1 tbsp of the balsamic vinegar.

2 Mix the lemon zest with the sugar and sprinkle over the strawberries. Finally garnish with the basil leaves and serve immediately.

Jordgubbstårta

STRAWBERRY GATEAU

FOR THE CAKE

4 eggs

330 g (11½ oz) caster sugar

180 g (6¼ oz) plain flour

2 tsp baking powder

100 ml (3½ fl oz) hot water

50 g (2 oz) flaked almonds, toasted until golden

FOR THE FILLING

200 ml (⅓ pint) *vaniljvisp* (Swedish vanilla whip), thick cold custard or pastry cream

250 g (9 oz) strawberries, hulled and lightly crushed

150 ml (¼ pint) whipping cream

TO DECORATE

250 g (9 oz) whole strawberries

SERVES 6–8

My birthday, being in the middle of July, coincides with the height of the Swedish strawberry season. When I was little it was far more common to cook using seasonal ingredients, and so a strawberry gateau was a must for my birthday. A wonderful cream cake with masses of strawberries really represents summer to me.

1 Preheat the oven to 175°C/350°F/gas 4. Butter and line a 23 cm (9 in) cake tin. Beat the eggs and sugar together in a large bowl until thick and pale. In a seperate bowl combine the flour and baking powder thoroughly, and fold carefully into the eggs and sugar. Finally add the hot water and the almonds and stir gently.

2 Pour the cake mixture into the cake tin and bake at the bottom of the oven for 30–40 minutes. The cake is ready when a skewer inserted into the middle of the cake comes out clean. Turn the cake out immediately and leave it to cool on a cooling rack.

3 Cut the cake in half horizontally. Spread the bottom layer with the vanilla whip, custard or pastry cream and top with the crushed strawberries. Place the other cake layer on top.

4 Whip the cream until stiff and spread over the cake to cover the top and sides. Decorate with the whole strawberries and serve.

Nötmarängtårta

HAZELNUT MERINGUE GATEAU

3 egg whites

110 g (4¼ oz) caster sugar

100 g (4 oz) hazelnuts, finely chopped

200 ml (⅓ pint) whipping or double cream

500 g (1¼ lb) fresh berries

SERVES 6

This hazelnut meringue is quick to make and goes beautifully with any seasonal berries. If you're making this in summer when strawberries, blueberries and raspberries are at their very best, definitely use fresh berries. If not, frozen berries will also work here.

1 Preheat the oven to 125°C/250°F/gas ½. Beat the egg whites with half of the sugar until stiff. Gently fold in the hazelnuts and the remainder of the sugar.

2 Draw a circle about 20 cm (8 in) in diameter on a piece of baking parchment and spoon over the meringue to fill the circle. Bake at the bottom of the oven for about 45 minutes, or until the meringue has set and coloured slightly. Remove from the oven and leave to cool.

3 To serve, whip the cream and spread on the meringue base. Decorate with the berries and serve immediately.

Blåbärspaj
BLUEBERRY PIE

150 g (5 oz) plain flour

140 g (4¾ oz) caster sugar

½ tsp baking powder

125 g (4½ oz) butter

2 tbsp cold water

250 g (9 oz) blueberries

1 tbsp potato flour or cornflour

TO SERVE

vanilla ice cream or custard

SERVES 6–8

During the summer months I often take my family to visit friends at their summer house in the Blekinge skerries on the south-east coast of Sweden. If we time our trip right, the wild blueberries that grow there are just ready to pick and we take a little boat out to the islands and come back with buckets full of berries. If we are too late there's still the 'berry man' who sells lingonberries and blueberries from the boot of his car in the town square.

The blueberries that grow in the Scandinavian woods are smaller and more intense in both flavour and colour than the ones you find in most supermarkets, which are sometimes so fat and juicy they're almost like grapes!

1 Mix the flour, half of the sugar and the baking powder together in a mixing bowl. Rub the butter into the dry ingredients and add the water. Mix together to form a dough then leave to rest in the fridge for 30 minutes.

2 Preheat the oven to 175°C/350°F/ gas 4. Set aside one third of the dough and press the remainder into a 20 cm (8 in) pie dish. Prick the pastry with a fork and bake blind for about 8 minutes.

3 Remove from the oven and tip in the blueberries. Sprinkle over the potato flour or cornflour (this will prevent the pie from becoming soggy) and the remaining sugar.

4 Roll out the reserved pastry. Cut into strips of around 2 cm (¾ in) wide and arrange on top of the berries. Bake for about 20 minutes or until the pie is golden brown. Serve with vanilla ice cream or custard.

Allemansrätt

Allemansrätt, the right of access to private land, is enshrined in Sweden's constitutional law, but in fact is not a law as such. It gives everyone the basic right to move freely over open land, with some conditions. It is designed to prevent people from fencing off forest, land or coast to prevent others from enjoying it. There are rules for what you may and may not do (like putting up a tent, or starting a camp fire in restricted areas), and what you can pick, but in general it offers an amazing opportunity for everyone to enjoy the glories of Swedish nature. You could almost call *allemansrätt* our cultural heritage, and it is thanks to its existence that Swedish 'picking' culture has survived: we can pick mushrooms or berries in any wood we like, and in the summer and autumn we Swedes head out en masse, armed with berrying baskets and mushroom knives.

Kanelbullar

CINNAMON BUNS

100 g (4 oz) butter

400 ml (14 fl oz) milk

50 g (2 oz) fresh baker's yeast

110 g (4¼ oz) caster sugar

pinch of salt

1–1.25 kg (2–2½ lb) plain flour

FILLING

3 tbsp butter

3 tbsp granulated sugar

2 tsp cinnamon

1 egg, beaten

3 tbsp sugar nibs

MAKES ABOUT 40

When my daughter Sara was young she used to love to help me bake these buns. Children seem to really enjoy kneading and shaping dough. Sara learned that, as with any sort of yeast baking, you should remember to use as little flour as possible for the quantity of wet ingredients. That's the way to get the best results!

1 Melt the butter in a saucepan over a medium heat. Add the milk and heat gently until it's lukewarm.

2 Crumble the yeast into a mixing bowl and pour over the milk and butter. Stir until the yeast has dissolved. Add the sugar and salt then mix in as much flour as is needed to make a smooth, springy dough. Cover with a clean tea towel and leave to rise for 30 minutes.

3 Knock it back and knead the dough until it is shiny. Halve the dough and roll out each half into a rectangle. Mix together the ingredients for the filling and spread half on each rectangle.

4 Roll up each rectangle into a long sausage and then cut each into 20 pieces. Put into paper bun cases and leave to prove for a further 30 minutes. In the meantime preheat the oven to 250°C/475°F/gas 9.

5 Glaze the buns with the beaten egg. Sprinkle over the sugar nibs and bake in the middle of the oven for 6–8 minutes, or until the buns are golden brown. Leave to cool on cooling racks.

Autumn HÖST

Autumn in Sweden

Slowly, slowly, autumn creeps up on us. The mornings are heavy with dew and night falls earlier as we linger over our last few suppers outdoors. School starts in the middle of August in Sweden, and the beaches empty as the birch leaves start to turn. In September there's a nip in the air, and come October it's time to roll up the garden hose, take down the clothes line and shut up the summer cottage.

And yet, because autumn kicks off with one of the most important events in the Swedish culinary calendar, the crayfish season, it doesn't feel sad at all. Crayfish means party time! It's also the season for the startlingly odoriferous *surströmming* (fermented herring), which is popular in the north. It's an aquired taste, to say the least, and to spare unwary readers I've not included the recipe for it here. On the west coast, September sees start of the Swedish lobster season, all very secretive at first (where best to drop the creels?) and then loudly festive. Of course, early autumn is also the best time to pick mushrooms. I find it so sad to see the pasty, packaged efforts on sale in the shops – just think how many mushrooms there are out there that taste so much better. As well as mushrooms, Sweden's forests offer another marvel for the deeply savoury dishes of autumn – lingonberries. Swedes eat truly astonishing quantities of lingonberries. These sharp berries are almost never eaten raw, but are cooked in any number of ways and eaten with everything from meatballs to fried herring.

With the nights growing longer and the autumn gales setting in, it's time to get snug indoors. I spend a bit more time in the kitchen and concentrate on stews and slow cooked food. All Saints' has recently become something of a foodie celebration. Perhaps it's because Halloween has now arrived to stay in Sweden, but many people take the opportunity to throw a party to brighten up the autumn darkness. It's so satisfying to lay the table for a dinner party in late autumn: candlesticks, some flourishes of ivy, conkers and glowing autumn leaves, and suddenly it's elegant and cosy. And it's worth seizing the opportunity to offer a really rich tart for pudding, crammed with autumn fruit – very welcome on a wet November evening.

Crayfish parties

A Swedish crayfish party is one of the very few traditional festive meals that doesn't involve herring. The reason crayfish ended up with their own celebration is that until 1994 it was forbidden to fish for them until the first Wednesday in August, whereupon everyone celebrated the 'crayfish première' by throwing a big party. Since most crayfish are imported these days, the law has been abolished, but many people still celebrate on this date. The crayfish are usually cooked in a broth that includes beer, masses of dill and plenty of spices. On the west coast people tend to prefer scampi, which have softer shells, and are often served gratinated with garlic butter. The expected accompaniments are a special spiced cheese, bread, beer and a very large amount of schnapps. Both the crayfish and the schnapps are honoured in any number of drinking songs, and according to tradition the party goers wear paper hats and sit outside or on their veranda, eating by the light of paper lanterns.

Västerbottenpaj

VÄSTERBOTTEN CHEESE TART

120 g (4½ oz) plain flour

100 g (4 oz) butter

2 tbsp cold water

150 g (5 oz) Västerbotten cheese
or other mature hard cheese

3 eggs

200 ml (⅓ pint) double cream

salt and freshly ground
black pepper

SERVES 4–6

No crayfish party is complete without a Västerbotten cheese tart. Crayfish on their own aren't terribly filling, and to survive the traditional onslaught of schnapps you need something more substantial to eat. This tart is also a nice addition to any buffet, and makes excellent individual pies for a picnic.

1 Whizz the flour, butter and water together in a food processor to form a dough. Press out the dough in a large pie dish, prick with a fork and refrigerate for 30 minutes or so. Meanwhile preheat the oven to 225°C/425°F/gas 7.

2 Coarsely grate the cheese. Beat the eggs and cream together, add the cheese and season to taste, bearing in mind that the cheese can be very salty.

3 Bake the base blind for 10 minutes, then pour in the cheese mix and bake the pie for a further 20 minutes until it's set and golden brown. Allow the pie to cool in the tin and serve cold.

Swedish cheeses

I am crazy about cheese! For a moment of heaven I visit Möllans Ost in my hometown, Malmö, where there is so much to taste and learn. They supply a large number of restaurants in the region and the owner, Peter, is really passionate about his profession. You can find Swedish cheeses in all varieties but most famous is probably Västerbottensost. It has been made in Burträsk in in the province of Västerbotten since the 19th century and is now a protected, registered trademark. It's a wonderfully balanced, matured hard cheese that lends itself perfectly to being eaten just as it is or used in cooking. Another Swedish cheese speciality is so-called 'breakfast cheese'. It's common to have a cheese sandwich for breakfast, and this early hour calls for thin slices of a bland cheese. Hence the invention of the Swedish cheese slicer – the perfect tool for thinly slicing cheese. It's such a common household object that Swedes who move abroad gasp in amazement when they can't buy it in their local shop.

Rotfruktsgratäng
POTATO AND ROOT VEGETABLE GRATIN

6 floury potatoes, thinly sliced

2 carrots, thinly sliced

1 small celeriac, thinly sliced

1 parsnip, thinly sliced

1 onion, thinly sliced

salt and freshly ground
black pepper

300 ml (½ pint) single cream

SERVES 4

Gratins are so cheap and simple to make. The mixture of root vegetables used here gives the finished dish a subtle sweetness that goes well with smoked, roast or grilled meat. As the vegetables need to be sliced very thinly you may find it easier to use a food processor, and the peelings can be reserved to make the Root Vegetable Crisps opposite.

1 Preheat the oven to 200°C/400°F/gas 6. Butter an ovenproof dish. Layer all the vegetables in the dish, seasoning between the layers.

2 Pour over the cream and bake for about 45 minutes in the middle of the oven until the vegetables are soft when tested with the point of a knife. Serve with smoked, roast or grilled meat.

Rotfruktschips med örter
ROOT VEGETABLE CRISPS

500 g (1¼ lb) clean, raw root vegetable peelings, such as potato, carrot, parsnip and beetroot

100 ml (3½ fl oz) rapeseed oil

salt and freshly ground black pepper

2 tbsp chopped fresh herbs of your choice

SERVES 4

I try to limit my kitchen waste as much as possible, and these crisps are the perfect way to use up vegetable peelings. When you make the root vegetable gratin opposite, don't throw away the peelings, make these crisps instead. They keep well and are a delicious, crunchy alternative to mass produced crisps that will wow your guests. Choose organic vegetables to avoid any pesticide residue on the skins, and scrub really well before peeling to remove earth and grit. The crisps are tastiest if the vegetables have been thinly peeled using a vegetable peeler.

1 Pat the peelings with kitchen paper to remove any excess moisture. Heat the oil in a large frying pan and fry the peelings a few at a time until golden brown and crispy. Be careful not to let them burn.

2 Drain the crisps on kitchen paper, or they'll be too greasy, and season. Sprinkle over the herbs.

3 Spread out on a baking sheet lined with baking parchment until ready to eat. Don't put them in a plastic bag as they will go soft and chewy.

Lingonsylt

LINGONBERRY JAM

500 g (1¼ lb) fresh or frozen
lingonberries

380 g (13 oz) caster sugar

MAKES ABOUT 1 LITRE (1¾ PINTS)

Lingonberries are verging on sacred for Swedes. In the autumn, market stalls have mountains of intensely-red lingonberries in wooden punnets, and many people go out into the woods to pick their own. Lingonberries taste similar to cranberries, and since they aren't sweet they provide a wonderful, tart contrast to many meat dishes. Lingonberry jam is at its very best when made by simply stirring the fresh berries with sugar. The sauce can then be frozen as it won't keep for long.

1 Pick over the berries and rinse well, or thaw if frozen. Put the berries in a mixing bowl and add the sugar. Stir with a wooden fork until the berries have become pulpy and the sugar has dissolved.

2 Spoon into sterilized glass jars and store for a maximum of 2 days in the fridge, or freeze in a suitable container.

Rödbetsinläggning

PICKLED BEETROOT

1 kg (2 lb) small whole beetroot,
scrubbed

75 ml (2¾ fl oz) Perstorps
24% *ättika* (acetic acid)

165 – 220 g (5½ – 8 oz)
caster sugar

**MAKES APPROXIMATELY
1.5 KG (3 LB)**

I like to make my pickled beetroots with small, tender beets. If the beets you have to work with are large, all you have to do is to slice them before pickling them. In Sweden the most common pickling vinegar is *ättika* (acetic acid) made by Perstorps, which should be handled with care. If you can't get hold of it use a similar pickling vinegar instead and follow the instructions accordingly.

1 Boil the whole beetroot in simmering water for about 30 minutes until soft. The small, tender beets don't need to be peeled but if using larger beetroots, scrub them well before boiling and peel them once they're cooked.

2 Pour the *ättika* (or similar pickling vinegar) into a saucepan. Add 550 ml (18 fl oz) cold water and the sugar and bring to the boil. Add the beetroot and simmer for a couple of minutes.

3 Decant into sterilized jars. Seal and leave to cool.

Senapsgurkor

PICKLED CUCUMBERS WITH MUSTARD SEED

2 kg (4½ lb) small cucumbers

150 ml (¼ pint) Perstorps 24% *ättika* (see page 179)

500 g (1¼ lb) caster sugar

50 g (2 oz) salt

3 blades of mace

2 tbsp yellow mustard seeds

3 heads of dill

5 cm (2 in) piece fresh horseradish, sliced

MAKES APPROXIMATELY 2.5 KG (5½ LB)

Since time immemorial we have eaten preserves of different kinds, traditionally as a way of storing food through the cold, dark winter. It's very simple to pickle your own cucumbers, and they make a perfect gift for Christmas or as a thank you present.

1 Place the cucumbers in sterilzed glass jars. Pour the *ättika* (or similar pickling vinegar) over the cucumbers and add 750 ml (1¼ pints) cold water along with the sugar and salt. Add the blades of mace, mustard seeds, dill and horseradish.

2 Seal the jars. Leave in a cool place for at least 3 weeks before eating.

Chanterelles

There is nothing quite like it. You've been searching for ages and suddenly you see that one yellow little hat that gives a whole group of golden chantarelles away – hooray! All Swedish children are taught from a tender age to recognize chanterelles, and once you've managed to find a good chanterelle spot in the woods, you keep it a dark secret from everyone except your nearest and dearest. Often you have to look long and hard, but it really is worth all the effort.

Every year, at the beginning of October, we travel to Småland, the next province north to my home, to visit family and to pick funnel chanterelles. Once the Swedish elk hunting season begins, no one in their right mind would go into the woods to pick mushrooms for fear of being shot, so we have to time our trip carefully! My brother-in-law, Peter, grew up in the Småland woods and knows them well, but even so he always takes a compass so we can be certain of the way home again.

In only a few hours we can pick anything from 5 to 10 kg (11 to 22 lb) of wonderful mushrooms each. The rest of the day is spent huddled in the kitchen, cleaning the mushrooms ready for drying. Once clean, we dry the mushrooms at room temperature on sheets of newspaper, then when winter comes we can enjoy the fruits of our autumnal labours and cook many wonderful dishes that will remind us of our day in the woods.

Trattkantarellsoppa med ostpinnar

FUNNEL CHANTERELLE SOUP WITH CHEESE STRAWS

2 tbsp butter

250 g (9 oz) fresh funnel chanterelles

1 banana shallot, finelly chopped

2 tbsp plain flour

1 litre (1¾ pints) vegetable stock

50 ml (2 fl oz) dry white wine

100 ml (3½ fl oz) single cream

salt and freshly ground black pepper

4 slices of day-old white bread

75 g (3 oz) Kvibille blue cheese (or other blue cheese) grated

SERVES 4

My daughter Sara, pictured opposite, has been picking mushrooms since she was very small. Even as a child she knew exactly how to clean our big harvest of funnel chanterelles and how to cut off the stalks without taking off too much of the mushroom. Handy skills for mushroom pickers!

1 Melt the butter in a saucepan and fry the chanterelles and shallot for a couple of minutes.

2 Sprinkle over the flour, stirring continuously, then add the stock a little at a time. Bring the soup to a simmer and cook gently for about 10 minutes. Add the wine and cream. Season to taste.

3 Preheat the grill to a medium heat. Cut the bread into slices and sprinkle with the cheese. Grill for about 5 minutes until the cheese has melted.

4 Serve the soup hot with the freshly baked cheese soldiers.

Gyllene kantareller med pasta och sparris

PASTA WITH GOLDEN CHANTERELLES

2 tbsp butter

350 g (12 oz) fresh
chanterelles, cleaned

1 bunch fresh asparagus, sliced

salt and fresly ground
black pepper

200 ml (⅓ pint) crème fraîche

50 ml (2 fl oz) dry white wine

1 tsp soy sauce

fresh pasta for 4 people

SERVES 4

Golden mushrooms fried in butter and served on wholemeal toast are simply sublime. But if you want to make more of a meal of your golden chanterelles, they are wonderful served with pasta. Pasta is, of course, not a Swedish invention but it is very much part of modern Swedish cooking. I've added asparagus in this recipe although it is usually harvested in spring, and, although less common, there is also a spring variety of golden chanterelles. So if you are lucky enough to get your hands on them, try making this dish in spring instead of autumn.

1 Melt the butter in a saucepan and gently fry the mushrooms and asparagus for a couple of minutes. Season to taste and pour over the crème fraîche. Add the wine and soy sauce and heat through.

2 Cook the pasta according to the instructions on the packet and serve immediately with the mushroom and asparagus sauce.

Porterstek 'Svärmors dröm'

BEEF BRAISED IN STOUT, OR 'MOTHER-IN-LAW'S DREAM'

330 ml (½ pint) stout

100 ml (3½ fl oz) undiluted
blackcurrant cordial

100 ml (3½ fl oz) soy sauce

6 black peppercorns

6 juniper berries

3 cloves of garlic, peeled

1 beef stock cube

1 onion, chopped into wedges

1 tsp chopped fresh thyme

1 tsp salt

2 kg (4½ lb) rump steak

5 tbsp plain flour

300 ml (½ pint) single cream

TO SERVE

boiled potatoes and steamed
seasonal vegetables

SERVES 8–10

'Mother-in-law's dream' is the common name for this beef dish that my granny often served when we went to her house for Sunday dinner. In my family we like to have a traditional Sunday roast as often as possible, gathering the family together for a big meal. It's a great oppotunity to catch up with everyone and relax before the hectic working week begins.

1 Mix the stout, cordial and soy sauce together in a heavy-based, lidded saucepan large enough to hold the beef joint. Add the peppercorns, juniper berries, whole cloves of garlic, stock cube, onion, thyme and salt. Bring to a simmer over a medium heat.

2 Add the steak. Cover and simmer for around 30 minutes until the meat is cooked, turning the meat over half way through cooking. Remove the steak and leave to rest, reserving the cooking juices.

3 Measure the cooking juices and add enough water to make the liquid up to 800 ml (1¼ pints). Return the juices to the pan. Sprinkle over the flour and whisk to remove any lumps. Add the cream and simmer, whisking continuously, for about 3 minutes. Pour the sauce over the beef and serve with boiled potatoes and steamed seasonal vegetables.

Skomakarlåda

SHOEMAKER'S BOX (BEEF AND MASH)

8–10 small floury potatoes

200 ml (⅓ pint) whole milk

4 tbsp butter

½ bunch of parsley, finely chopped

salt and freshly ground black pepper

100 g (4 oz) smoked bacon, chopped

600 g (1½ lb) sirloin steak

SERVES 4

There are many stories about why this dish is called 'shoemaker's box', but it is likely to be because the dish it is served in looks rather like a shoe box. The ingredients vary from recipe to recipe, but the basis of all versions is meat, which represents the sole of a shoe (although it should absolutely not be as tough!), and bacon, which is the nails or tacks used by shoemakers. This is a real Swedish classic that tastes delicious.

1 Boil the potatoes in lightly salted water until just cooked. Drain and steam dry.

2 Warm the milk and add a little at a time to the potatoes while whisking, using a hand-held electric whisk, until the potatoes form a firm mash. Whisk in 2 tbsp of the butter and add the parsley. Season to taste.

3 Dry fry the bacon in a frying pan until crisp and set aside.

4 Melt the remaining butter in the frying pan and fry the steak on a high heat for a couple of minutes on each side (depending on how you like your steak cooked). Deglaze the pan with a splash of water.

5 Serve with the mash at the bottom, the meat in the middle and a sprinkling of bacon 'tacks' on top. Spoon over the cooking juices from the frying pan.

Viltgryta
GAME STEW

2 tbsp butter

600 g (1½ lb) game, such as venison, diced

8 small onions, halved

100 g (4 oz) fresh funnel chanterelles, or equivalent in dried mushrooms

salt and freshly ground black pepper

4 juniper berries, crushed

2 tbsp gin

100 ml (3½ fl oz) cream

3 carrots, sliced

TO SERVE

boiled rice and Apple Jelly (see page 205)

SERVES 4

A hearty helping of this game stew with a glass of good red wine can't fail to cheer up a dark autumn evening. Choose the game according to the hunting season, availability, and, of course, taste. The stew benefits from being made in advance and then reheated.

1 Melt the butter in a large casserole over a medium heat. Add the meat and cook until browned, then add the onions and mushrooms and fry until just beginning to colour. Season to taste and add the juniper berries.

2 Pour 200 ml (⅓ pint) water into the casserole and add the gin and cream. Cover and simmer on a gentle heat until the meat is tender. The exact time will depend on the type and cut of meat, but this should take between 30 minutes and one hour.

3 Add the carrots to the stew for the last 5 minutes of cooking time. Serve with boiled rice and Apple Jelly (see page 205).

Sjömansbiff

SAILOR'S BEEF
(BEEF, POTATO AND ONION STEW)

2 tbsp butter

600 g (1¼ lb) stewing steak, thickly sliced

1 large onion, sliced

8 medium waxy potatoes, thickly sliced

3 carrots, thickly sliced

salt and freshly ground black pepper

330 ml (12 fl oz) stout

2 tbsp bottled beef stock concentrate

2 bay leaves

½ bunch of parsley, chopped

TO SERVE

Pickled Beetroot (see page 179) and Pickled Cucumbers with Mustard (see page 180)

SERVES 4

There must be many Swedes who remember this dish from the Sunday dinners of their childhood. The whole dish is cooked in one large casserole, which worked well in a ship's galley, which is where the name comes from. Carrots aren't included in the original recipe, but I think they make it even better. Pickled Beetroot (see page 179) and Pickled Cucumbers (see page 180) are traditional accompaniments.

1 Melt the butter in a large casserole over a medium heat. Add the meat and cook until browned, then add the onion and fry until beginning to colour.

2 Add the potatoes and carrots and season. Pour over the stout and stock concentrate, and add the bay leaves. Bring to the boil and simmer over a low heat for 40–50 minutes until the meat is tender and the potatoes are soft.

3 Sprinkle over the parsley and serve with the pickled beetroot and cucumbers.

Fläskfilé med en ton av pepparrot

COLD ROAST PORK WITH A HINT OF HORSERADISH

2 tbsp oil

1 tsp soy sauce

salt and freshly ground black pepper

600 g (1¼ lb) pork tenderloin

FOR THE MARINADE

50 ml (2 fl oz) oil

50 ml (2 fl oz) dry white wine

1 tbsp sweetish mustard

freshly grated horseradish, to taste

25 g (1 oz) toasted flaked almonds

SERVES 4

When you're feeding a crowd it's good to be able to prepare everything well in advance, otherwise you don't get the chance to talk to your guests. I like to roast whole pork tenderloins that I then marinate and serve cold. Depending on the season, I pair the pork with a potato or pasta salad. This recipe is easy to multiply if numbers demand it.

1 Preheat the oven to 175°C/350°F/gas 4. Mix the oil and soy sauce together and season, then brush on the pork tenderloin.

2 Roast the pork in the oven about 20 minutes until it's cooked through. Remove from the oven and leave to cool.

3 Thinly slice the pork and arrange neatly on a serving dish. Mix the marinade ingredients together and drizzle over the meat. Leave to stand in the fridge for at least 2 hours.

4 Scatter the grated horseradish and almonds over the meat and serve as park of a buffet.

Kåldolmar

STUFFED CABBAGE ROLLS

75 g (2 oz) pudding rice

20 white cabbage leaves, hard stalks removed

5 tbsp butter

1 onion, chopped

150 g (5 oz) pork mince

150 g (5 oz) beef mince

2 eggs, beaten

150 ml (¼ pint) milk

salt and freshly ground black pepper

50 ml (2 fl oz) golden syrup

TO SERVE

boiled or mashed potatoes and Lingonberry Jam (see page 176)

SERVES 4

Stuffed cabbage rolls are traditional daily fare in many Swedish homes. In southern climes, dolmades made with vine leaves stuffed with different fillings are eaten, and this Swedish version calls for typical local ingredients such as cabbage and minced beef with lingonberry jam as the accompaniment of choice. Pick a rainy autumn day to sit indoors making cabbage rolls, for they do take a while to prepare. Make extra and freeze a few so they are ready to whip out of the freezer on busy weekdays for a quick but wholesome meal.

1 Cook the rice in water according to the instructions on the packet and leave to cool. Preheat the oven to 175°C/350°/F/gas 4.

2 Bring a large saucepan of lightly salted water to the boil and blanch the cabbage leaves, a few at a time, until soft. Drain well. Heat 2 tbsp of the butter in a saucepan and sweat the onion until translucent.

3 Mix the minced meats with the egg, milk, cooked rice and onion to form a fairly loose stuffing. Divide the stuffing between the cabbage leaves, roll up tightly and pack into an oven-proof dish.

4 Drizzle over the syrup and dot with the remaining butter. Bake for about 30 minutes.

5 Add a splash of water towards the end of the cooking time to make a gravy. Serve hot with potatoes and lingonberry jam.

Rårakor med bacon

POTATO CAKES WITH BACON

8 medium waxy potatoes,
coarsely grated

2 Hamburg parsley roots,
coarsely grated

1 egg, beaten

salt and freshly ground
black pepper

150 g (5 oz) smoked bacon,
chopped

2 tbsp butter

TO SERVE
Lingonberry Jam (see page 176)

SERVES 4

Potato cakes are traditonally made using potato as the only vegetable, but I love it when the taste of Hamburg parsley cuts through. Together with the smokiness of the bacon and the bitter-sweet lingonberry jam, it's a happy combination. If you can't find Hamburg parsley, it can be substituted with any other root vegetable you fancy.

1 Mix the grated potatoes and Hamburg parsley together with the beaten egg and season well.

2 Dry fry the bacon in a frying pan. Drain on kitchen paper and set aside. Melt the butter in the frying pan and drop in spoonfuls of the potato mix. Fry over a medium heat until the cakes are soft on the inside and golden brown on the outside.

3 Top with the bacon and serve with lingonberry jam.

Helstekt spätta

WHOLE FRIED PLAICE

4 whole plaice, gutted and
heads removed

salt and freshly ground
black pepper

60 g (2¼ oz) plain flour

4 tbsp butter

12 mushrooms of your
choice, sliced

16 large cooked prawns, peeled

TO SERVE

lemon slices and boiled potatoes

SERVES 4

If you get the chance, it's worth buying whole, fresh plaice straight
from the boat, or at least as fresh as possible. I think it's best
served straight from the pan with potatoes, mushrooms and
prawns. Simply delicious.

1 Season the plaice and coat in the flour. Heat half of the butter
in a large frying pan and gently fry the fish until the flesh is firm
and white.

2 Meanwhile heat the remaining butter in a seperate pan.
Add the prawns and cook until they begin to turn pink. Add the
mushrooms and cook for a further 2 minutes.

3 To serve, put the fish on warmed plates and top with the
mushrooms and prawns. Garnish with lemon and serve with
boiled potatoes.

Torsk med rotsaker

COD WITH ROOT VEGETABLE MASH

600 g (1¼ lb) floury potatoes, halved

2 Hamburg parsley roots or other root vegetables, chopped

600 g (1¼ lb) thick cod fillet

3 tbsp rapeseed oil

salt and freshly ground black pepper

150 ml (¼ pint) milk

1 tbsp butter

zest and juice of 1 lemon

4 sprigs of dill

8 cherry tomatoes, finely chopped

100 g (5 oz) smoked salmon, cut into strips

5 cm (2 in) piece fresh horseradish, grated

SERVES 4

Root vegetables are at their best in the autumn, and this root vegetable mash makes a change from ordinary potato mash. Cod is one of my favourite fish, but there are issues over sustainability in some areas. If it is on the 'red list' in your country, use any other firm white fish instead.

1 Preheat the oven to 150°C/300°F/gas 2. Cook the potatoes and Hamburg parsley (or other root vegetables) in lightly salted water until soft.

2 Meanwhile divide the fish into four portions. Brush with 1 tbsp of the oil, season and place in an ovenproof dish. Bake in the middle of the oven for 10–15 minutes until the fish is just cooked.

3 Drain the vegetables well. Add the milk and butter and season to taste. Mash the vegetables using a hand-held electric whisk.

4 Whizz the remaining oil, the lemon zest and juice and 3 sprigs of the dill together in a food processor to make a dressing. Stir in the tomatoes and season to taste.

5 Divide the mash between warmed plates and place the fish on top. Top with the smoked salmon, drizzle with the tomato dressing, sprinkle over the horseradish and remaining dill and serve.

Löjromstoast

KALIX LÖJROM CANAPÉS

150 g (5 oz) Kalix löjrom
(vendace roe)

4 pieces of really good bread

4 shallots, finely chopped

4 tbsp crème fraîche

SERVES 4

Having seen just how little roe there is in each vendace, and how much work goes into washing it, I am not in the least surprised that the price is so high. Add in the fact that it tastes amazing, and it all makes eminently good sense! Vendace roe is usually sold frozen, and if you are lucky to have a pot stashed away in the freezer, you can pretty much dig it out with a spoon without thawing it if you suddenly fancy a bit of luxury on toast, or want to garnish a piece of fish.

1 If frozen, thaw the roe in the fridge. Toast the bread until golden, butter and slice each into four triangles.

2 Spoon a little crème fraîche onto each piece of toast, then a spoonful of the roe and finally a sprinkling of shallot. Serve immediately while the toast is still crisp.

Fikonchutney

FIG CHUTNEY

400 g (14 oz) fresh figs, chopped

zest and juice of 1 lemon

2 tbsp muscovado sugar

5 walnut halves, chopped

**MAKES 400–500 ML
(14–18 FL OZ)**

In the autumn, we usually get masses of figs on the tree that grows in our greenhouse. Figs generally don't survive the Swedish winters, even as far south as Skåne, and while we eat as many fresh ones as we can, they don't keep for long, so we make chutney with the rest. This chutney is superb with meat dishes, but also with a nice bit of mature cheese.

1 Place the figs in a saucepan. Bring to a simmer over a low heat and add the lemon zest and juice, then mix in the sugar.

2 Simmer, uncovered, for about 10 minutes. Stir in the walnuts and leave to cool, then pot in sterilized jars and seal. The chutney can be stored in the fridge for about 2 weeks.

Björnbärssylt

BLACKBERRY PRESERVE

2 kg (4½ lb) blackberries

1.5 kg (3 lb) granulated sugar

MAKES ABOUT 2.5 LITRES (4½ PINTS)

On a beautiful autumn day when the sun is shining, there's nothing I enjoy more than blackberry picking. This blackberry preserve makes a perfect accompaniment to Rice Pudding and Rice Cream Pudding (see page 48).

1 Put the blackberries in a saucepan and heat gently until they begin to release their juice. Bring to the boil and allow the blackberries to simmer in their own juice for 10 minutes.

2 Remove the pan from the heat and stir in the sugar. Leave the preserve to cool and thicken, stirring occasionally. Skim the surface.

3 Spoon into sterilized jars and seal. Store in the fridge or freeze in a suitable container.

Äppelgelé

APPLE JELLY

2 kg (4½ lb) apples
(preferably crab apples)

1 kg (2 lb) granulated sugar
per litre (1¾ pints) juice

**MAKES ABOUT 2½ LITRES
(4½ PINTS)**

In September, the apple trees in the orchards of Skåne groan under the weight of their colourful fruit and there's no better time to make this delicious apple jelly. Crab apples are perfect for this – although the small, slightly sour apples make horrid eating, they make superb jelly. If you can't get your hands on crab apples, use cooking apples instead. This jelly is delicious with roast meat or pâté.

1 Prepare the apples by cutting off any blemishes and removing the stalks, then chop the apples without peeling or coring (retaining the cores and skin will add flavour). Put the chopped apples in a large saucepan or preserving pan and pour over 2 litres (3½ pints) water. Bring to the boil, cover and reduce the heat. Simmer over a low heat until the apples are just beginning to go soft and pulpy (the time taken will vary according to the size and type of your apples).

2 Strain the fruit and juice through a jelly bag or muslin cloth and leave to drain thoroughly. Don't squeeze the apple pulp or the finished jelly will be cloudy.

3 Measure the strained juice, pour back into the saucepan and cook for 5 minutes. Measure the amount of sugar needed for the quantity of juice and add to the pan. Stir over a gentle heat until the sugar has dissolved.

4 Bring to the boil and simmer for 10 minutes, skimming off any scum that rises to the surface. Test for set by dipping a dry spoon into the jelly – if it sticks to the spoon, the jelly is ready.

5 Spoon into sterilized jars and store in the fridge.

Here I am with my brother and father under the big apple tree in my grandparents' garden in the early 1960s. My grandparents had huge orchards and I loved visiting them to help my father collect apples.

Min skånska äppelkaka

MY SKÅNE APPLE CAKE

6 medium eating apples, cored
and thinly sliced

4 tbsp butter

50 g (2 oz) breadcrumbs

110 g (4¼ oz) golden caster sugar

60 g (2¼ oz) flaked almonds

TO SERVE

Vanilla Custard (see below)

SERVES 6

When autumn comes, the time to make apple cake is upon us. This version is typical for Skåne, my part of the world, but there are probably as many recipes as there are cooks. Let this one inspire you to create your own masterpiece. Cold Vanilla Custard (see below) is pretty much essential, but whipped cream comes a close second.

1 Preheat the oven to 200°C/400°F/gas 6. Butter a 25 cm (10 in) ovenproof dish. Arrange the apples in the dish and sprinkle over the breadcrumbs, sugar and finally the flaked almonds.

2 Dot with the remaining butter and bake in the centre of the oven for about 30 minutes until the cake is golden brown. Serve with cold Vanilla Custard (see below).

Vaniljsås

VANILLA CUSTARD

2 eggs, separated

2 tbsp caster sugar

200 ml (⅓ pint) whipping cream

1 tsp vanilla sugar

zest of ½ a lemon

SERVES 4–6

I like to make this sauce to go with my various fruit pies and crumbles. It goes just as well with rhubarb crumble in spring as it does with apple cake in autumn.

1 Beat the egg yolks and sugar together until thick and pale. In a seperate bowl whisk the egg whites until stiff, and in a third bowl whip the cream to soft peaks.

2 Fold the cream and egg whites into the egg yolk and sugar. Add the vanilla sugar and lemon zest and serve.

Hjortronstrutar

CLOUDBERRY AND CREAM CORNETS

30 g (1¼ oz) icing sugar

1 egg white

30 g (1¼ oz) plain flour

½ tsp vanilla sugar

25 g butter, melted and cooled

200 ml (⅓ pint) *vaniljvisp* (vanilla whip) or vanilla ice cream

6 tbsp cloudberry jam

SERVES 6

While I was at university in Umeå I came to realise why cloudberries are called Norrland's gold – the golden berries ripen in the autumn and glitter like jewels in the great woods and moors of this region. They taste indescribably wonderful, and presented in these sweet cornets they're good enough to serve just as they are, standing in individual glasses.

1 Preheat the oven to 200°C/400°F/gas 6. Draw 6 circles measuring 12 cm (4¾ in) in diameter on two or three sheets of baking parchment.

2 Whisk the icing sugar and egg white together until stiff. Carefully fold in the flour and vanilla sugar so there are no lumps but the mixture remains fluffy. Finally add the cooled, melted butter.

3 Spread the mixture into each of the circles on the baking parchment and bake in the centre of the oven for about 5 minutes. Keep an eye on them as you don't want them to burn. Remove from the oven and immediately roll into cornets. Place each in a drinking glass to set.

4 Whisk the vanilla whip until fluffy, or let the ice cream soften a little, then fold in 4 tbsp of the cloudberry jam and use this to fill the cornets. Top each with a dollop of cloudberry jam and serve immediately.

Hasselnötsmuffins

HAZELNUT MUFFINS

300 g (11 oz) shelled hazelnuts

6 eggs, separated

330 g (11½ oz) caster sugar

3 tbsp breadcrumbs

1.5 tsp baking powder

½ tsp vanilla sugar

MAKES ABOUT 40

These fantastic hazelnut muffins are smaller than those often served at cafés and coffee shops, and make for a more dainty treat. I have my mother to thank for this recipe, which has cheered up many a rainy autumn afternoon.

1 Preheat the oven to 200°C/400°F/gas 6. Grind the nuts or whizz in a food processor until finely chopped but not oily.

2 Beat the egg yolks and caster sugar together until thick and pale. Fold in the nuts, breadcrumbs, baking powder and vanilla sugar. Beat the egg whites until stiff and fold carefully into the nut mixture.

3 Fill paper cases two-thirds full with the muffin mix. Bake in the centre of the oven for 8–10 minutes. Test with a skewer to check that they're done.

Hasselnötsmuffins   c:a 40 st.

6	st.	ägg
3	dl.	socker
3	msk.	skorpmjöl
300	gr.	hasselnötskärnor
1,5	tsk.	bakpulver
2	"	vaniljsocker

Rör äggulor och socker poröst, tillsätt

nötterna blandade med skorpmjölet samt

bakpulvret.

Blanda sist ner de till skum slagna vitorna.

Gräddas i 200 gr. 8 min.

A Swedish larder

I'm so lucky to live in Sweden, where I have a fantastic landscape on my doorstep and the opportunity to get fresh food from farmed lands, woods and seas. The climate in the south of Sweden allows me to grow wonderful vegetables in my beloved garden close to the sea, but I also live close to the big foodhalls of international and multicultural Malmö.

As a cookery author and food journalist I always have too many things in my storecupboard, and I conduct new cooking experiments almost every day. My garden also serves as my storecupboard and it's wonderful to be able to just step outside to pick tomatoes, rhubarb and herbs in summer.

I always stock up on whatever is in season. Fresh ingredients are essential and I like to stick to seasonal produce as much as possible. However, as Swedish winters can be rather long, I do sometimes have to rely on my freezer to keep me in a good supply of berries and vegetables. If you have the space, try and freeze the fresh fruit and vegetables you have bought locally during their natural harvesting season instead of relying on those that have travelled from another part of the globe.

Pasta and rice may be commonplace in Sweden these days but nothing beats the good old potato when it comes to traditional cooking. In winter I always make sure I have lots of potatoes and root vegetables in my larder. Swedish cooking uses a lot of dairy products and I always keep a good supply of butter, cream and milk in the fridge.

The shelf I use for pickled vegetables, jams and chutneys is usually groaning under the weight of many jars at the beginning of autumn. I can't go though the rest of the year without these accompaniments. And as it's impossible to celebrate most Swedish festivities without some kind of herring, you will usually find some type of pickled herring or anchovies hidden in a corner. Somewhere close by you will probably find a bottle of schnapps.

If you look into any Swedish larder I would safely gamble on that you'll find these two things: lingonberry jam and crispbread. You certainly will in mine!

Stockists

IKEA
Kingston Park
Fletton
Peterborough PE2 9ET
08453 583363
sales.shoponline@ikea.com
www.ikea.com

SCANDINAVIAN KITCHEN
61 Great Titchfield Street
London W1W 7PP
020 7580 7161
info@scandikitchen.co.uk
www.scandikitchen.co.uk

SWEDISH PRODUCTS
87 Dyne Road
London NW6 7DR
08453 017 685
www.swedishproducts.co.uk

A TASTE OF SWEDEN
4 High View Road
Ipswich
IP1 5HJ
01473 430460
info@atasteofsweden.co.uk
www.atasteofsweden.co.uk

TOTALLY SWEDISH
32 Crawford Street
London
W1H 1LS
020 7224 9300
shop@totallyswedish.com
www.totallyswedish.com

Index

Acknowledgements

I'm so grateful to my mum who was a splendid cook and encouraged me to taste varied food as a child. Of course I was not always so happy when she came home with many bags of raw herring or chicken and taught me how to handle these foods from scratch! But as the years have passed I've really learnt to appreciate all the things she taught me and all the use I've had from this knowledge in my job.

Thankfully my husband Per and my daughter Sara always volunteer to test my newly-developed recipes. They have become really good at cooking themselves and nowadays they give me lots of inspiration.

I also want to thank Tine for being so patient during my cooking and styling, waiting to take the perfect shot for this book, and thanks to Petra, who has been the bridge between the Swedish and English languages and cooking habits.

Picture credits

Margareta Schildt Landgren: pages 28, 29, 32, 33, 46, 47, 73 (top right), 109, 161, 169, 185, 206 (middle right) and 213.

Alamy: page 210.